A KIND OF LIVING SCRAPBOOK

by
DICK EMERY

Extracts from the Scripts by
JOHN WARREN AND JOHN SINGER

Foreword by DONALD ZEC

Illustrated by STANLEY FRANKLIN

FUTURA
PUBLICATIONS LIMITED

A Futura Book

First published in Great Britain in 1973 by Robson Books Ltd.

First Futura Publications edition 1974.

Text Copyright © 1973 Dick Emery.

Extracts from the scripts Copyright © John Warren and John Singer.

Forward Copyright © 1973 Donald Zec.

Illustrations Copyright © 1973 Stanley Franklin.

The Publishers acknowledge with thanks the co-operation of the BBC. Acknowledgements are also due to British Lion Films for the photographs of Dick Emery, Hettie, Lampwick, Mandy and Mr Partridge; and to the Daily Mirror for the photograph of Donald Zec.

ISBN 0 8600 7078 6

Printed and bound in Great Britain by
REDWOOD BURN LIMITED
Trowbridge & Esher

DICK EMERY

IN CHARACTER

Contents

*To my darling wife Jo
and to Peter
for all the laughs we've had*

Acknowledgements

I would like to take this opportunity to express my sincere appreciation to John Stanley who helped to get this book off the ground; to Bill Cotton who made it all possible; to scriptwriters John Warren and John Singer; producer Colin Charman; costume designer Velma Buckle; dresser Joe Howe; make-up girl Cherry Alston; and indeed to all those who have worked so zealously with me on *The Dick Emery Show*.

D.E.

Foreword

Donald Zec

There are certain entertainers I can happily take or leave. Occasionally, when a limp performance has positively begun to droop, it produces within me a lethargy so overpowering it's almost too much to reach for the switch.

It is then that one closes the eyes and prays for a power cut.

But then there is the reverse of the coin. A power cut smack in the middle of a gem of a performance by a master of the craft.

This particular catastrophe once occurred to the nation in the case of that many-faceted genius, Mr Dick Emery.

Now, I can take (or leave) a misfire at Cape Kennedy. You may dangle me without warning in a crippled cable car over an Alp. But to pull the switch on this incomparable entertainer, to halt him in his tracks just a titter away from the terminal, must be the biggest misuse of power since Genghis Khan.

I like Dick Emery. Correction. I love him.

Deep inside his densely populated mind lurk some of the most preposterous—but highly recognizable—characters that ever pimped, pouted, or solicited their way into universal favour. Those who disagree with me can probably be counted on the fingers of one hand—like Harvey Smith's.

As with the best clowns—Chaplin, Morecambe, Sellers, Jack

Benny—Emery's humour is merely the tip of the iceberg. Invisible but formidable is the actor beneath, with a sharp eye, an alert ear and a superb sense of timing. Without all this, his characters wouldn't be worth two penn'orth of greasepaint. But with this somewhat sawn-off genius at the controls, the roles are as flawless as the Burton diamonds.

If 'Can I do you now, sir?' was the catchphrase of the Forties, 'Ooh, you are awful—but I like you!' is clearly its tele-equivalent of the Seventies. Taken by itself, this may not be the most seductive statement since that one about reducing prices at a stroke. But delivered by Mandy, that brassy, falsied trollop with the beehive hairdo and last night's eye-shadow—the phrase has a built-in bawdiness all of its own.

And then there is Lampwick, the doddering relic of World War One, with a cough out of an Army Nissen hut at dawn. And nervous, sex-starved Hettie, hungrily grabbing anything that is male and moves. And the gallery of stiff-legged colonels, frail gentlewomen, the bovver-booted, the queer, the priestly and the peers of the realm. Mr Emery handles them all with the touch of the master (or mistress), aided by brilliant scripts known in the BBC as 'The Emery Papers'.

The fact that one very successful feature film based on the TV series has already appeared and that another is about to be made, confirms Emery's immense popularity with the millions. His impersonations of women, right down to the last pout, shrug or petulant sniff, are as deadly accurate as his camp characters with their prissy walk, sly giggles and salmon-pink trousers. Even Emery concedes that it might beg the question: is he a man or a mousse?

Well, he has been married five times, has four children, can fly his own plane and take a car engine to pieces, and are there any further questions?

He has been married for the last two years to a tall, attractive and talented dancer, Josephine, who gave up her career, devoting herself entirely to nurturing this kind and complex entertainer.

Like almost every clown in the business, the strain of battling for the laughs has Emery swinging between elation and acute despair. 'I'm a terribly difficult person to live with,' he says. 'Most comics are. We're a tensed-up lot. We live on our nerves, and if the audience doesn't fall about, we get sick to the stomach. One minute you're all lovely and relaxed, the next you're worried about the game, worried about where the next job's coming from, just worried . . .'

Even though he's been at it for twenty-five years?

'Makes no difference,' he says. 'As one show finishes there's always the next challenge staring you in the face. Remember I've had a lot of starvation in this business. And I mean literally, like the day my Mum and I were down to half a loaf and a tin of baked beans. Luckily I got a job at the Windmill. I phoned my mother and said, "Get some meat on tick, we're going to eat".'

His father was an entertainer, and so was his mother until Emery was born. 'She had me while Dad was appearing at the Palladium. She phoned him and said, "Laurie, I feel a song coming on"—that was me.'

During the toughest years, Emery's fears and phobias drove him to long sessions with hypnotists and analysts. 'I had a chip on my shoulder just like my Dad did, God rest his soul. And it doesn't pay to have a chip when you're an entertainer . . . I was frightened of producers, of managers, petrified of failing, terrified of being dumped as a flop. But finally I found out what made me tick, asked myself questions and came up with the right answers.'

The success of his impersonations is based on truth, his flair for looking at people and not missing a trick. Travelling 40,000 miles a year, Emery's piercing eyes are always alerted, looked for new characters, or subtle variations on the old.

So if you see him coming your way—duck. For I should warn you that anything you say, or do, may be taken down and used—and not necessarily to your advantage.

The Author

A Kind of Living Scrapbook

Introduction

To ask a man to write about himself seems to me to be an open invitation to self-deception, self-congratulation and ego-fanning. Net result: the boredom of a considerable portion of the readership. To invite me to piece together a composite picture of each of my favourite characters and to try to trace their individual conception and development looks to me like publisher's suicide! However, at the risk of making a fool of myself, let me invite you to join me in this attempt to unravel something of the backgrounds of each of my infamous friends.

In a succession of newspaper, radio and television interviews over the years, I have been asked from where I derive my characters, which is my favourite, whether I associate myself with any particular one of them. All good questions, but within the confines of a newspaper column or a few minutes on the air, quite impossible to answer, and so I have tended to work out in advance a selection of amusing and evasive replies designed to keep the interview moving without touching seriously on these areas. Even now, with so many pages at my disposal, I'm not sure how best to explain the emergence of Mandy, Lampwick and the Bovver Boy. They have become such separate identities in their own right that to look at them afresh and try to trace their parentage feels as much an attack upon personal liberty as if a private report were being made upon myself.

Where, then, did it all start?

I was literally born into the business. My father was a variety artist and so right from the beginning I wanted to go on the stage. At first my ambition was to be a serious opera singer, and during my teens I did work as diverse as farming, car driving and journalism in order to earn enough money to take proper singing lessons with the Italian Chekko Mattania. In some small way I still wish I could have developed such talent for singing as I had, but fate beckoned me in other directions. I have always believed that throughout life we are offered opportunities, and it is up to us to spot and take advantage of them. If I had missed the chance to enter the field of entertainment, I would almost certainly have worked with cars in some way or another, and had I missed that opening too—well, who knows what I should have turned out to be? One of my characters, perhaps!

The first time I performed in character, I was nineteen and working in a summer concert party, as they were called in those days, in Minehead. Officially I was the Assistant Stage Manager and light comic, and I went on with an act in which I portrayed two characters, an idiot and an old gardener. Strange how playing elderly people fascinated me, even then. I once saw an act in which a troupe of young male dancers were dressed up as old men, and yet were going through a routine that would have killed most athletes. I found that very funny, and have used the idea in the character of Lampwick, who isn't averse to 'having a go' at someone who ruffles him, despite his apparent age. The fun is not meant unkindly, and being incongruous, Lampwick's actions are therefore rather endearing.

Before that summer show started, my mother sat in the empty theatre for the best part of two weeks drilling me on entrances and exits, which are a vital part of playing characters: think, for example, of Mandy's trip as she minces off, or the Old Colonel swinging his wooden leg around the corner, or the Bovver Boy shuffling up to the camera. Movement is integral in the building up of a convincing character, and after a time, as with Mandy's trip, it can become the physical equivalent of a catchphrase.

A lot of nonsense is talked about the business of characterization. It is simply a matter of observing and relating. We've all seen women like Hettie, the man-mad spinster with spectacles and just one thing on her mind. But what makes her convincing on the screen isn't just her obsession—it's the way she holds her shoulders, pulls her mouth down, and anxiously clutches her handbag. The skill lies in sifting out the key characteristics so as to emphasize her mannerisms without making a caricature of her. And if you are playing a character on stage, rather than on television, the approach may have to be different, even though the character might look the same. You have to reach across the lights to the audience in a big theatre, so the make-up and costumes and gestures have to be given that much more emphasis. The difference is even more apparent in the delivery of lines. Mandy, for instance, is coy in manner in her television appearances, but on stage she is a much harder nut.

I was brought up in the era of the marvellous Chaplin films and he has always been a major influence on me. To my mind, he has no equal. There is nothing new in comedy, whatever people and papers may claim, and there will always be someone to replace you—contrary to what many people in show business might think, we are all very replaceable. Chaplin is the only exception. He is unique in being irreplaceable. I especially admire his ability to mix pathos and humour, and over the ten years of my TV series I have wanted to create an Emery Theatre rather than a comedy show. Don't get me wrong—I'm not trying to wring mileage out of that cliché about the clown yearning to be a straight actor! What I mean is, I would like to create a show in which I can develop the sad and endearingly pathetic sides of these characters, which are the perfect foil for humour—just as Chaplin did. In the last series we managed quite a successful compromise with such sketches as the one where Lampwick finds himself ousted from his proud position as British Legion standard-bearer, or the one where he overhears his daughter and son-in-law discussing how to get rid of 'the old thing' because he's past it. The audience—and Lampwick—are led to believe that they are talking about him, but at the end we realize that they've been discussing the budgie. The formula engages the audience's sympathies at the same time as it makes them laugh.

I hope to be able to explain the origin of each of my characters, but just as a child needs a parent to help it form and develop, so I need help and guidance in forming and developing my characters. I am fortunate in having round me a skilled team who help to fashion the raw concept into a well-rounded and polished act which is both entertaining and convincing. Indeed, it might be that the scriptwriters and the producer contribute more to this than I. I don't say this to please them, but because sometimes the characters have originated in their minds rather than in mine. What is certain is that, however and by whomsoever the character is conceived, the writers John Warren and John Singer give it shape and depth before passing it over to me to interpret. At this point, Colin Charman, the producer, helps me to develop the performance within the framework of the cameras and the time available.

In addition, I have a resident team of make-up girl, costume designer and dresser who time and again—often under terrible conditions—turn me out on a filming day just as though I were a child being packed off to school. Working from caravans or make-shift dressing-rooms, we have managed as many as a dozen costume and make-up changes in a morning, and filmed each on a separate street location. In the process, the characters have become real people to us all. I find that I think in a totally detached manner about each. For instance, if I'm considering possible script material for the Bovver Boy, I find that I'm reading it in the persona of Dick Emery, but assessing it *in character*, as something the Bovver Boy might fancy—or take a thundering dislike to, and possibly tear up!

It's difficult to say how these sketchy characters which are scripted, dressed, lit, rehearsed and filmed, take on flesh and blood and materialize as real people in my imagination, and I hope, in my projection of them on the screen. Certainly, I do know, given a set situation, how any one of them would react. This stems from my own belief in the character's identity; without my total involvement, the character would be nothing but a hollow shell, and would convince no one. Fortunately, I have a good memory which enables me to 'dig up' individuals I have met in the past upon whom a character might be modelled and on whose reactions I might draw.

Almost all the characters have their basis in reality since they are largely modelled on people I have known—a kind of living scrapbook of my own encounters. For instance, there is the Duchess, a character whom we have not used for a while. She may seem far-fetched, with her faded elegance and blue-tinted hair, but she isn't hard to find living in retirement along the South Coast. The Duchess was based on a woman who employed me as her chauffeur at a time when I was trying to earn extra money to pay for my opera singing lessons. Also, I had always loved cars, so when I learnt that a chauffeur was required for a very high-class car, I applied double-quick. The woman and her husband lived in fashionable Hampstead; to her great satisfaction he was a colonel and a Conservative MP. I had to wear the former chauffeur's uniform; unfortunately his head was two sizes larger than mine, so I would drive my dignified cargo of passengers around with my head held high—and my cap stuffed with newspapers to keep it from falling over my eyes! And Madam insisted that it was only right and fitting, in view of her husband's exalted status, that I should salute the Master each time he alighted from the car. At that point, I understood why the previous chauffeur had left, and swiftly followed suit.

There is no excuse for that kind of snobbery. Every man has his dignity, which has nothing to do with the man-made wealth and power structure of society—I hope this dignity is apparent even in my characters. From then on I begin to resent such high-handed behaviour. So it was that lady from Hampstead who provoked me to sharpen my chisel and carve out the figure of the Duchess, while my dancing instructress, Flora, an enormous woman pushing six feet tall and with quite the largest bust I've ever seen, provided the voice. 'Dear little Dickie,' she would cry, bearing down on me like a stormtrooper. Funnily enough, the first time I played the Duchess character was in Michael Bentine's marvellous TV series, *It's a Square World*, a decade before my shows even began. It just goes to show the odd ways in which a woman can get under—and stay under—your skin!

Living alongside these characters for in some cases as many as twenty years creates a bond of friendship and a respect for them and their way of thinking. Luther Fritton, for instance, the straw-chewing, gap-toothed, besmocked farmer who appears from time to time, charms me with his earthy good humour and lack of pre-tension. In fact, there is only one character who feels quite unreal to me—I'll tell you why later. And there is just one for whom I feel particular affection, and of whom I could say, 'At a given moment in life, that might almost be me!'

One thing I ought to mention here is my attitude towards drag. For some reason it is always my female characters' punchlines which people remember and greet me with when I am out in the street. I have only to walk down a railway platform to be greeted with

Mandy's 'Ooh, you are awful—but I like you'. Indeed, as I walk to the train, I often feel that people expect me to do Mandy's trip and then walk bow-leggedly away, as she does on television! I would be rather less than honest if I didn't admit that I enjoy being recognized and chatted to by the public. We are all extroverts in show business—you have to be—but I must say that I resent being called after in the street by people wanting to know where my handbag or skirt is. I realize that it's meant good-naturedly, but I have never set out to be a female impersonator. Real drag is only for artists like Danny La Rue, who can look genuinely glamorous and lady-like. I could never match his brilliance and glamour. I am primarily interested in putting across character rather than in achieving a totally successful feminine appearance. What I try to be is a character actor working funny situations rather than a comedian dressing up, whether it be as a male or female.

To me, my family of characters reflects various aspects of the British way of life. Over the years they have become close and hardworking friends. I hope that you will spend some time with me now while I introduce you to my household of familiar faces, and perhaps then you might know a little more about me, too.

INTERVIEWER   *Ah, now here's a charming young lady . . .*
MANDY   *Hullo.*
INTERVIEWER   *Tell me, have you ever been presented with an opportunity that could change your life?*
MANDY   *Oh, yes. Only last week, my boss called me into his office and said he had something in mind that would do me a lot of good.*
INTERVIEWER   *You, mean, something that would enlarge your prospects?*
MANDY   *. . . Pardon?*
INTERVIEWER   *Something that would tickle your fancy?*
MANDY   *Ooh, you are awful . . . But I like you!*

THE TON-UP BOY

The Ton-Up Boy

The Ton-Up Boy

I have always loved mechanical things. I spent my childhood earnestly studying the performances of the British motor bikes which were so triumphantly successful at the TT races. Men like Stanley Woods were my heroes, and to me Britain's true glory and achievement lay in the noise and smell of machines like the Norton rather than in the more traditional splendours of our way of life.

I am passionately interested in motor cycles. I learnt to ride in a field on a motor bike that only continued to fire from sheer habit—it was that old and decrepit. A little later, during my stint at the famous Windmill Theatre, my career took a small financial turn for the better, and I bought a BSA A7, astride which I fulfilled my childhood dreams and hurtled about London feeling like a king.

The sensation of riding headlong into the wind on a powerful machine which obeys your least touch is an exhilarating one, and remains at the core of the attraction of motor cycling, though fashions in gear and bikes may come and go. I get a surge of pleasure just from watching a rider roar off on his motor bike, his dollybird clinging behind on the pillion. The young motor cyclist gets a great kick out of that combination of power and skill, and as long as he's not causing trouble or endangering others, I wish him luck.

Although I am now an avid motorist, and am fortunate enough to be able to run the cars of my choice, I still regularly use a motor

cycle—in fact, most of the bikes used in the series have been mine. Once when I rode my bike to the film location at Ealing, a stranger came up and apropos of nothing asked me to take the Ton-Up Boy out of the shows, since he felt that the character was spoiling the image of the sport and its enthusiasts in general. Bless him he and thousands like him take their hobby very seriously and are the stalwarts of this national interest. However, I must insist that I have never intended to ridicule motor cycling enthusiasts through this character or make them the butt of our fun. Neither, conversely, do I play him because I am mad about motor cycling, but simply because he represents a recognizable individual who can be seen on any city street—a convenient peg, in fact, on which to hang a funny situation or dialogue.

Towards the end of the last series, the Ton-Up Boy was treated to occasional excursions on a piece of high-status machinery: a chopper. Although it looks so powerful and is complete with high-handled bars and much shiny chrome-work, it is in fact an unusual 50cc Italian moped called a Fantic. Other bikes which he rides, such as the 750cc, can out-pace even my wife's E-Type.

He needs little in the way of make-up, except for the thick wig. In addition to his basic motor cycling gear, his jacket is adorned with chains and badges, and he wears a military helmet. These singularities are, I hope, suitably representative of the aggressive individuality which such young men like to assert. In a way, this preoccupation of the young enthusiasts with looking distinctive is a whip for their own backs, for the accepted outfit of black leather, denims and goggles has come to represent to the public the uniform of a troublesome minority, and motorcyclists in general have been saddled with an unfortunate reputation which belongs to the few who would probably cause trouble whether they were riding a motor bike, working on the factory floor or studying at university.

I have met many motor cycling enthusiasts over the years at trials, races, clubs and cafés around the country. I have watched them and been amazed at their dedication to their machines. Indeed, I sometimes think that a true fanatic's bike is more important to him than his girl—it certainly gets far more attention! He knows every inch of it, and keeps it in tip-top condition always.

I once opened the National Motor Cycle Exhibition, and as I was being escorted round, we passed through a coffee bar crammed with motor cyclists of all ages. Separated from the rest of the crowd by a distinct gap was a group of hard-faced would-be Hell's Angels, who glared balefully at me as I stood signing autographs. I didn't blame them; I was only frivolously incidental to the show as far as they were concerned. Yet enthusiasm is catching, and when I spoke to them about their bikes we were soon engrossed in discussion. Those unsympathetic to their interest might find their manner and coarse jokes menacing, but it is only their all-or-nothing attitude to what is after all a man's hobby: if you're not interested, go away! To a fellow motor cycling enthusiast, however, they are just eager fanatics. Personally, I like their straightforward honesty about what interests and what bores them.

The Ton-Up Boy has been a member of my television family from the earliest series. He is still happy-go-lucky, full of the kind of jokes he might have picked up from the group's last gathering, and above all dedicated to his bike. He is no invention of mine, but as likely as not one of those enthusiasts from that Exhibition coffee bar.

INTERVIEWER	*Pardon me, sir.*
TON-UP BOY	*Wotcher, son.*
INTERVIEWER	*Tell me, do you come from a big family?*
TON-UP BOY	*Oh, yer. I got loads of brothers and sisters. Smashing lot, they are.*
INTERVIEWER	*Would you describe your family as tight knit?*
TON-UP BOY	*Not half. The old man's always tight and mum's a nit!*

INTERVIEWER	*Excuse me, sir.*
TON-UP BOY	*Yeah, son?*
INTERVIEWER	*Tell me, do you find there is a strong community spirit in your neighbourhood?*
TON-UP BOY	*Fantastic, that's what it is, fantastic. Take what we've done for Charlie the window cleaner. He fell off the ladder and broke his arm. There he was, poor old soul, wearing 'imself out trying to carry on one handed.*
INTERVIEWER	*Oh, what a shame.*
TON-UP BOY	*Yeah, he just wouldn't stop work—so us lads stepped in and helped him out.*
INTERVIEWER	*You mean, you cleaned the windows for him?*
TON-UP BOY	*No, we broke his other arm.*

TRAFFIC WARDEN

Traffic Warden

Traffic Warden

Here is a character only too familiar to most of us, especially to those who live or drive in our larger towns. Instantly recognizable in his navy and yellow uniform, he stalks the pavements with the measured, meaningful tread of a man ever conscious of the weighty burden of civic responsibilities laid upon him.

The petty officials of this world are not restricted to men in uniform—they're just easier to portray that way. The effect of a uniform on a man's character is well known, whether he be brass bandsman, policeman, council worker or in the armed forces. Yet it still amazes me how, merely by donning a uniform, a nice ordinary person can change from a decent human being into a kind of automaton, programmed only to give and take orders, a self-styled overlord above the common run of humanity. It's not so much an attitude, more a dedication to higher things than being a civilized human!

I know it by experience. During the last war I had a very good mate. His bed was next to mine in the dormitory; we got on famously together, went out together, drank together—until one morning a notice was pinned on the board announcing that he had been made a corporal. Within twenty-four hours he was a changed man. Those two stripes set him apart from and above the rest of us. Henceforth we were all less than the dust beneath his feet.

I can't forgive that kind of thing. It seems to me that true

authority does not reside in the number of bands or stripes sewn onto a jacket, nor does it manifest itself in a bullying attitude towards those of inferior rank. I saw too much of this kind of thing during my time in the forces, but at least it provided me with background material which later I would draw upon when creating and developing characters in uniform.

My Traffic Warden is the product of many years' watching and disliking such characters. He is the vicious, bullying type who never knows when to turn a judicious 'blind eye'. But although his origins lie in a kind of pot pourrie of men in uniform, his voice and attitude belong to the character I played in Peter Brough's great radio programme in the Fifties, *Educating Archie*. I was Monty, a clever, know-all character since adopted by—and even acclaimed as the trade mark of—a number of other comedians. I do not mind; they do say that imitation is the sincerest form of flattery . . . In the ensuing years, my Monty has grown into this petty Corporal of the Pavements who appears regularly in the show.

I sometimes play an altogether different character in uniform, however, called Crump. He sometimes appears as a traffic warden, sometimes as a park attendant. Crump is a very dejected, depressed and miserable little man. He has a tiny moustache and a far-away look which complement his abject apologies just for *being* there: 'I can't help it . . . it's my job.' At least you can feel sorry for this man in uniform. His apologetic attitude towards his job colours our view of it, and he is a far more sympathetic character than the authoritarian Traffic Warden.

A satchel and the all-important note-pad and pencil are the Traffic Warden's props. His uniform is standard issue, and his make-up is minimal. To achieve that aggressive expression I jut out my lower jaw and adopt a sternly quizzical frown, as though permanently challenging the motorist's right to park—or even own—his car! I also wear a very mean, regimented moustache. Pacing up and down with the Traffic Warden's measured, steady rhythm helps me to slip into his frame of mind.

What are they like when they get home, I wonder. Do these officious wardens continue to persecute those around them? Are they still conscious of the heavy burden of duty? Or do they kick off their shoes and become the complete family man, kind and indulgent? Theirs is a hard job, there is no doubt, and they are on

37

the receiving end of much blame and abuse. Their reputation for pettiness probably stems from a mixture of the motorist's frustration at not being able to find parking space, and the attitude of those wardens who patrol the streets like mine does, dedicated to the downfall of the motorist at all costs.

In some towns where the warden's beat is severely restricted, like Manchester, where there are only eight meters to a warden, boredom and frustration must set in very early in the day, and God help the motorist who even has the temerity to drop off a passenger, let alone try to park! In other places, like Kingston-upon-Thames, the balance of meters to wardens is much more favourable to the motorist, with one warden per sixty-five meters. Not only does this give the motorist a more even chance, it also means that the warden's beat is that much wider-spread and more interesting to patrol.

Perhaps the reason why some wardens are more officious than others is a throwback to their formative years, when they were bullied and pushed about and sneaked on. Now they discover that by donning a warden's outfit, the roles can be reversed. Their uniform compensates for their character deficiencies. Imagine such a warden's first day on the beat—it must be like those advertisements where the seven-stone weakling suddenly gains a massively powerful body and is naturally eager to show off his new-found strength!

Sometimes, while waiting for filming to start, I lounge about in my Traffic Warden's uniform and smoke or chat to the make-up girl, and I often wonder what impression of British wardens I must be giving to tourists. The least I can hope is that they don't go back home thinking that English traffic wardens all wear make-up on duty!

ENEMY Nº 1

SCENE: A typical lecture room, with several rows of chairs facing a raised dais on which stands a large object covered by a Union Jack. Hanging on the walls are various traffic signs and instructional material for traffic wardens. There is a door upstage right. Eight of the chairs are occupied by five women and three men in wardens' uniforms.

The door upstage flies open, and Crouch, a male warden, enters and comes to attention with military precision.

39

CROUCH Wardens . . . wardens . . . 'shun!

(The class leaps to attention as Dick, as Chief Traffic Warden, enters. He also is dressed as a warden, but with the addition of gold braid on his cap, double yellow lines round his sleeves and several medals dangling from his right breast. Dick and Crouch march in step to the dais and stand one on each side of the flag-shrouded object)

CHIEF Carry on, Crouch.

CROUCH Sah! Class . . . class . . . salute!

(They all come to the salute as Crouch slowly pulls off the flag to reveal a traffic meter. He conducts as they all sing in unison to the tune of 'Hi Jig-a-Jig')

ALL 'The meter, the meter, the baskets can't beat her,
No matter what drivers may say,
When they have found one that's free, we defeat 'em —
We cover it up straight away.'

(Crouch puts a 'Not in Use' bag over the meter)

'Singing . . .
Double yellow line, very heavy fine,
We love to hound 'em, the motorists' terror are we,
Write 'em out a chit, shake 'em up a bit,
We just adore it — our mothers weren't married, you see,
Bom bom.'

CHIEF *(wiping his eyes)* The Warden's Anthem. Always moves me to tears, it does. That and 'They're Digging Up Father's Grave' are a couple of classics, I reckon. Well, now, class, as you know, you are rapidly approaching the end of your training course, so I propose to devote this period to a quick recap of some of the basic principles. Can anybody tell me what is the main function of the warden?

(A male warden raises his hand)

CHIEF Yes, Bulstrode?

BULSTRODE To assist the motorist at all times and do everything possible to speed the flow of traffic through congested areas.

CHIEF Wrong!

BULSTRODE But that's what it says in the handbook, Chief.

CHIEF *(scathingly)* The handbook! A blind put out to deceive the stupid nellies. Now, you've all been sworn in under the Official Secrets Act, I take it?

ALL Yes, Chief.

40

CHIEF   Check the door, Crouch.

(Crouch hurries to the door, opens it and glances outside)

CROUCH   All clear, Chief.

CHIEF   Right. *(He surveys the class severely)* I am now going to reveal to you the true purpose of the Corps of Wardens. It is . . . to clear the roads of this Great Britain of ours of a pestilential scourge known as—the motorist!

(He flings out an arm dramatically as Crouch pulls down a roller to reveal a picture of a man with a handlebar moustache, wearing a cap, a club scarf and driving gloves. He grins over a steering wheel which he holds in front of him. Bulstrode, carried away, leaps to his feet, shaking his fist)

BULSTRODE   'Singing . . .
Double yellow line, very heavy fine—'

CHIEF   That's enough, Bulstrode. Take a grip, lad. Save it for the High Street.

CROUCH   Take note of the salient features: cap, scarf, driving gloves and a soppy leer.

CHIEF   It is him and his rotten ilk who must be driven off the roads and back into the garage where they belong.

(A dolly bird warden puts up her hand)

DOLLY BIRD   May I ask why, Chief?

CHIEF   *(with an oily leer)* A very intelligent question, darlin', and if you'd like to stay behind after class I'll be happy to expand on it. Tell 'em the answer, Crouch.

CROUCH   Last year, twelve million motorists paid twenty-five pounds a head into what is laughingly known as the Road Fund. A fraction of that money was actually spent on the roads.

CHIEF   Exactly. A state of affairs which we cannot allow to continue. If there were no lousy motorists to wear 'em out, we wouldn't need no roads at all. And that three hundred million quid could be put to a better purpose.

CROUCH   Like what, Chief?

CHIEF   Like employing more wardens for a start. Now, you may ask, how do we achieve this idyllic state? I'll tell you. By fair means or preferably foul. Harassment is one of our main weapons.

CROUCH   *(to one of the male wardens who is grinning broadly)* What are you smiling at, Johnson? Wipe it off. Who ever heard of a warden smiling?

CHIEF   Quite right. The most we permit ourselves is a slight snigger when slapping a ticket on a hearse outside an undertaker's.

CROUCH And in such cases, please remember to use the proper ticket provided. The one with black edges.

CHIEF Now, in order to assist you to obtain the proper number of persecutions . . . I mean, prosecutions—we have prepared one or two little visual aids. The first idea was submitted by a Barnstable warden who obtained an immediate award of the MC. *(He taps a medal on his chest)* The Motorist's Curse. Right, Crouch. *(Crouch switches on a large TV)* Here you see a typical example of the species known as the Meter Feeder . . . *(On the screen we see a small man sidling along a row of cars parked at meters. He reaches his own car and glances furtively around)* Notice his nasty, furtive approach and his cunning expression . . . *(The man produces a coin from his pocket and makes to put it in the meter, which is adjacent to a pillar box. The coin goes in the slot and the meter indicator goes back to two hours. The man smiles in sly triumph and starts to turn away. A hand comes out of the slit in the letter box and taps him on the shoulder. The man turns. The hand presents him with a parking ticket. The man takes it with a look of chagrin and exits. A passer-by pauses briefly to ram a rolled-up magazine into the letter box. As he walks on, the top of the letter box rises and Dick, in warden's uniform, stands up with the magazine protruding from his mouth like a Churchillian cigar)* A good warden must be prepared to suffer in the course of duty. *(We see Dick, in uniform, standing by a car at a meter which is about to go into excess. He has his notebook poised and is chewing bubble gum languidly)* The next little film is a very good illustration of the warden's First Commandment—Do Not Wait for a Motorist to Commit an Offence—Force Him To!! *(The same small man approaches the warden with a large grin. He looks at the still unexpired meter and looks delightedly at his watch)* This obnoxious specimen is Cocky Charlie. He's got about thirty seconds left on the clock and knows that once he gets in that car you can't touch him. He baits you. *(The man grins, holds up his ignition key and waves it in Dick's face, while he glances pointedly at the meter. Dick grins mirthlessly back. He blows a large bubble, removes the gum from his mouth and waggles it at the man. The man's expression suddenly changes to one of alarm. He makes a dive at the lock with his key but is forestalled by Dick's thumb which deposits the wodge of sticky gum all over the lock. The man struggles desperately to insert his key, but to no avail. With a 'thunk' the meter goes into the red. With a flourish, Dick completes a parking ticket, tears it off, and, grinning evilly, slaps it on the windscreen)* That little ploy earnt a warden from Ipswich a free pleasure trip round a car breaker's yard. Now we come to the ladies, bless 'em. *(He indicates a particularly sour-faced female)* Look at Warden Ironmonger there. My gawd, with another

42

fifty like her I'd take on London Transport. There wouldn't be a bus left on the road.

BULSTRODE *(putting up his hand)* We're not allowed to do them are we, Chief?

CHIEF Unfortunately no. And by the way, a word of warning. Do not muck about with Rolls Royces.

BULSTRODE But isn't that class distinction?

CHIEF Yes.

POLLY BIRD *(raising her hand)* Anything else we should watch out for, Chief?

CHIEF Well, I'll give you the cautionary tale of Warden Eager on the Westminster beat. He slapped a ticket on a big black car in Buckingham Palace Road with no number plates and a flag on the bonnet. He got a quick whack on the nut with a polo stick and was last seen buffing up Traitor's Gate with a tin of metal polish.

CROUCH Shall I roll the next film, Chief?

CHIEF Carry on, Crouch. Now, the next little wheeze is best left to our feminine comrades. *(We see on the screen the entrance to a car park controlled by automatic barriers. A motorist drives up, inserts a coin, the barrier rises and he enters. The barrier falls behind him)* Here you see the bane of our existence, the legal off-street parker. What, we ask ourselves, can we do to wipe the smirk off his face? *(We see on the screen Dick, as a female warden, standing by the car park entrance. The same little man drives up and puts a coin in the slot. We see the barrier go up. Dick lets out a wolf whistle. The man turns his head. Dick coyly raises his skirt to show an expanse of leg. The man takes an appreciative eyeful and gives Dick the 'thumbs up' sign. The man revs the engine and drives forward. The barrier descends with a grinding crash on the bonnet of the car. The watching class applauds involuntarily)*

CHIEF *(raising a modest, restraining hand)* Thank you, class. Well, on Monday morning you will be launched upon the streets as fully-fledged wardens. I only ask of you one thing—do your worst. And I leave you with this thought:

'The man who drives a car today
Is every warden's easy prey,
Just place your foot upon his bumper,
And shove a ticket up his jumper.'

CROUCH Class . . . class 'shun!

CHIEF *(saluting)* Carry on, and good luck. *(Exits)*

(The class begins to chatter. The door opens and the Chief re-enters)

CHIEF   Anybody going past Acton Vale?

BULSTRODE   I am, Chief.

CHIEF   Good. Those dirty, rotten, stinking coppers have towed my car away.

HETTIE

Hettie

Hettie

'Are you married?' I ad-libbed that all-important question in a girl's phrase-book (especially Hettie's) in a light-hearted script rehearsal, and from that moment the line became the inevitable conclusion to her weekly appearances. While the interviewer struggles for an answer, Hettie dives in and pins him up against a hedge, fence or wall.

For a long time Hettie was simply described as 'Frustrated Spinster', but although her mannerisms may be representative of this genre of female, she is in fact minutely modelled—even down to the name!—on one particular woman I once knew in the course of my work. Because the woman had access to the scripts, we couldn't list the character as 'Hettie' in case she recognized herself.

This woman used to wear long pleated skirts and huge blue, upswept, butterfly-wing glasses with diamanté frames. And she was *very* man-conscious. One day the make-up team produced a wig which looked exactly like the real Hettie's hair, and found amongst the wardrobe department's costumes one of those pink see-through blouses which were then so fashionable. Real-life Hettie actually saw the wig and blouse and remarked how like her own they looked! When she left the room, I was dressed up as her replica and encouraged to add the character to my repertoire. Fortunately the lady mostly lives abroad, but she does return to this country on odd occasions, and I cannot help wondering whether she has seen the resemblance yet.

Hettie, though ridiculous, is also a pathetic character. I try to bring out this side of her through movement and posture. The way she clutches her bag as though it were likely to be snatched from her at any moment makes her vulnerability palpable, and the way her shoulders droop and her rapid, nervous gait, too, bring out the pathos in her. (If you watch people standing or walking about, you soon notice how revealing of character their movements are. Shuffling, striding or mincing, head bowed or shoulders back or bottom swaying, a person's carriage is often an infallible guide to character.) When she is approached by the interviewer, Hettie becomes a very tense little woman, suddenly aware that she is the centre of attention. Such is her total preoccupation with finding a man that she reduces everything to terms of her own obsession, and finally her eagerness gets the better of her and she is quite carried away.

Her lipstick is applied in order to emphasize the narrow, bitter mouth with which she pulls such characteristic grimaces. Hettie is always filmed in sequence with Mandy, the blonde. All the make-up required to hide my masculine bristles is applied and we shoot Hettie first, leaving her make-up as the basis for Mandy's. Hettie's wig is specially made, and her spectacles might have come out of the real Hettie's handbag, so similar are they to the original pair! Her clothes of course are very frumpy, like her accessories.

I suppose she takes about ten minutes to make up, which sounds quick, but these sessions are always done under pressure, and Cherry, who has made me up for years, can produce miracles in no time at all, as can Joe, my dresser. Sometimes, when trying to make up and dress in a tiny caravan with an intrigued public hovering about on the other side of the flimsy curtains and the film crew impatiently pacing up and down, funnier situations occur than happen on the screen!

In Luton once, when I was dressed as Hettie and waiting on a street corner to start filming, a lady coo-eed loudly and waved vigorously at me, mistaking me for someone called Dora. It makes me wonder if the original Hettie finally cottoned on to my impersonation and hurriedly changed her name!

INTERVIEWER	*Excuse me, madam.*
HETTIE	*Miss.*
INTERVIEWER	*Miss. Do you believe that some men are better than others?*
HETTIE	*I don't know. I've never had the chance to find out. Are you married? I'm looking for a nice young man . . .*

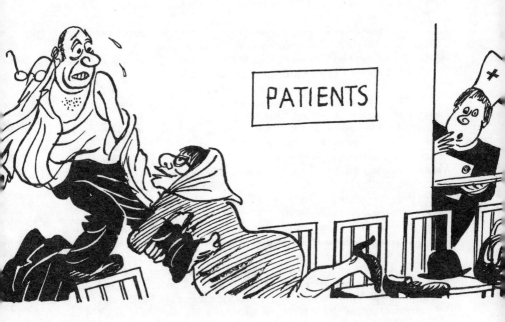

SCENE: A hospital waiting-room. There are many rows of empty chairs. A solitary man sits on the end chair of the front row nearest the door. He has a small holdall in front of him at his feet.

Dick enters, dressed as Hettie. 'She' is wearing a headscarf and street coat, and carries a handbag. 'She' looks round the waiting-room, spots the man and walks over to the empty seat next to him.

51

HETTIE Excuse me, but is this seat taken?

MAN *(uneasily)* Er, no, it's not taken.

HETTIE *(sitting down)* Oh, good! *(She fidgets)* Sorry to bother you, but would you mind moving a bit?

(The man moves his chair a few inches away from hers)

MAN How's that?

HETTIE No. I meant *towards* me. Never mind, I'll move *mine* instead. *(She shuffles her chair right up close to his)* Are you going in or coming out?

MAN Going in. I'm having my operation this afternoon. What about you, are you having one?

HETTIE *(looking down at the front of her coat)* Oh, no. It's just the way this coat hangs.

MAN *(embarrassed)* No, I meant are you having an *operation?*

HETTIE Oh, no, but I had one here a little while ago. I was in here for three weeks. It all started when I collapsed in the street. I had these terrible pains in my back. I lay there for hours until the ambulance arrived. And when it did, the ambulance men started arguing.

MAN *(interested)* What about?

HETTIE Well, I needed the kiss of life but neither of them wanted to give it to me.

MAN So what happened?

HETTIE Well, they finally gave me a mirror and told me to give it to myself. *(Sniffle)*

MAN *(concerned)* That's a fine way for ambulance men to behave.

HETTIE Anyway, they drove me here and carried me into the casualty ward. And the doctor on duty . . . well, I don't think he liked me.

MAN What makes you say that?

HETTIE Because he took one look at me and said to the ambulance men, 'Just because this hospital is named St George's, there's no need to bring in a sick dragon.'

MAN That's not a very nice way to talk about a sick dragon . . . er, patient.

HETTIE *(dreamily)* Ooh, he was gorgeous, though. He looked into my mouth and said, 'I'm afraid I'll have to take your tonsils out.' And I said, 'Well, if you're afraid, leave my tonsils where they are and take *me* out. I can be ready in ten minutes.' He said, 'I'm a happy married man.' So I said, 'That's all right, I'm an unhappy single girl and you know how opposites attract.'

MAN Hmm. Well, I don't reckon much to the staff here if that's the way they behave. From what I've heard, they're more interested in having orgies than helping sick people get better.

HETTIE *(interested)* Orgies? What orgies? *(She grips his arm)*

52

MAN	Well, there was one last night in the staff hostel. The gate porter was telling me about it. Sometime during the night a man broke into Matron's room and tried to . . . er . . . er . . .
HETTIE	Really? Some people have all the luck.
MAN	*(prises her hand away)* What?
HETTIE	Oh, nothing. Where was I?
MAN	You were saying about what happened after you'd been brought here and the doctor examined you.
HETTIE	Oh, yes. I *knew* you'd be a good listener. You've got sympathetic eyes. Your wife's very lucky to have such an understanding husband.
MAN	Actually, I'm not married. *(Emotionally)* I don't think I ever will be. My fiancée finished with me last night.
HETTIE	Oh, I *am* glad. *(Enthusiastically)* I mean, I'm sorry to hear it . . . Oh, you know what I mean. *(She swings her leg over his lap)* It's lucky I came along.
MAN	*(aghast)* Please! *(He pushes her leg off)*
HETTIE	Oh, sorry, I got carried away. Where was I?
MAN	Er . . . you were saying about the doctor.
HETTIE	Oh, yes. Well, he sent me to a specialist and the specialist gave me a complete examination . . . all over. And all the while I could see he had that certain look.
MAN	What look is that?
HETTIE	I felt he was dressing me with his eyes. He told me I needed transplants for every part of my body except my lips.
MAN	Why not your lips?
HETTIE	Because they've never been used. *(She puts her arm around him)* But you could soon put that right, couldn't you? *(She puckers up to him)*
MAN	*(breaking free)* Please don't do that!
HETTIE	Ooh, sorry, I got carried away again. By the way, what's wrong with you? What have you got to have operated on?
MAN	I'd rather not say.
HETTIE	*(nudging him)* Oh, go on. You can tell me. *(She winks)* Is it . . . *(She whispers in his ear)*
MAN	Oh, no, *that's* all right.
HETTIE	Well, what about . . . *(Whispers again)*
MAN	No, *they're* all right, too. *(Pause)* Perfect vision in both of them.
HETTIE	Well, what *are* you having operated on, then?
MAN	*(hesitantly)* Well, if you promise to keep it to yourself . . . You won't tell anyone?
HETTIE	My lips are sealed. Boy Scout's honour. *(She does a two-finger Scout salute)*

MAN   *(amazed) Boy Scout's* honour?

HETTIE   Yes, they wouldn't let me join the Guides so I joined the Scouts. But go on, what are you having your operation for?

MAN   Well, it's . . . *(He whispers in her ear)*

HETTIE   *(loudly)* Removal of a tattoo? Where from? *(The man reacts with embarrassment)* Don't worry, I'll find out for myself! *(She grabs his shirt and starts pulling it open. The man pushes her away)*

MAN   I've told you before about this. Leave me alone!

(Hettie suddenly gets pains in her back. She lies face upwards across his lap)

HETTIE   *(moaning)* Oh, my back, my back!

MAN   *(panicky)* W-w-what can I do to help?

HETTIE   *(painfully)* Help me up . . . but be careful, I'm very delicate.

(He struggles to help her up)

MAN   Is that better?

HETTIE   Yes, but it's still agony. Can you massage it for me?

MAN   *(aghast)* M-m-massage it?

(She grabs his arms and puts them over her shoulders so it appears that they are in a romantic clinch)

HETTIE   Now gently massage my back. Ooh, the pain, the pain.

(The man reluctantly massages Hettie's back)

MAN   How am I doing?

HETTIE   *(dreamily)* Ooh, lovely. Aren't you strong . . . and so gentle too.

(She puts her arms around him and holds him tight. The door opens and Sister enters)

SISTER   Nurse Grusesome! What's the meaning of this?

(The man breaks free from Hettie. Hettie jumps to her feet)

HETTIE   Ooh, sorry, Sister!

MAN   *(incredulously to Sister)* Did you say *Nurse*? She's a *nurse*? Here?

(Hettie is removing her coat and headscarf to reveal a nurse's uniform and headgear)

SISTER   *(glaring at Hettie)* Yes, she is, and she should've been on duty ten minutes ago.

HETTIE   I was only trying to cheer him up, Sister.

54

SISTER Well, now that you've cheered him up, take him into B Ward and get him ready for his operation. *(Exits)*

HETTIE Come along, I'll soon have your clothes off.

(The man struggles, but she has too firm a grip on him)

MAN No, please. I can't stand any more from you. Let me go! Leave me alone!

(She drags him out through the door)

INTERVIEWER	*Could you spare a moment, madam?*
HETTIE	*Miss.*
INTERVIEWER	*Miss. May I ask, do you think one should help one's neighbours?*
HETTIE	*Oh, yes. I live next door to the rugby club. Their dressing-room got burnt down last month, so I let all those big beastly men use my bedroom to change in.*
INTERVIEWER	*That's very kind of you. I expect you'll miss them when their dressing-room has been rebuilt.*
HETTIE	*Not for long. I'm going to burn it down again!*

LAMPWICK

Lampwick

Lampwick

Of all my characters, Lampwick is my favourite. Indeed, I feel that Lampwick might be myself—given a more advanced age and a different environment. He's been with me a long time, on stage and radio, in television and the cinema, and I feel that it is to him that I owe the increased popularity of the show over the last couple of years.

You see, I had always hoped to enter the world of character acting through my television shows, but my hopes were not fulfilled until I managed to change the format of the programmes, which originally consisted of quick sketches and musical interludes. The opportunity came with the *Grand Prix Special*, a fifty-minute TV programme in which I played Lampwick throughout, appearing as my other characters in little intervening sketches. The story-line concerned ageing motor ace Lampwick's determination to win one more race before marrying his long-suffering betrothed. This was great fun; we shot all the location material at Snetterton race circuit in Norfolk.

While I drove Lampwick's original ancient racing car, my rivals—chief among them Graham Hill!—drove modern Formula Ford single-seaters.

This show proved successful, and as a result the format of all the subsequent shows was changed—the musical side was dropped in favour of more lengthy character sketches.

So now you see why I feel a debt of gratitude to the old boy!

In spite of his cunning streak, Lampwick is endearingly straight-forward and *British* in the old-fashioned sense. If he saw an injustice, he would not hesitate to put his fists up and 'have a go', clucking away all the while and choking in the attempt to give vent to his indignation. He is also a Chaplinesque figure, a character whose potential for comedy is matched by his potential for pathos, who can turn suddenly from the ridiculous to the sublime, and back again.

Why Lampwick engages the sympathies of the audience so completely is difficult to say; after all, as a race we British are not noted for our compassion towards old people. But whether he is presented as the aged father tolerated (just) by his daughter and son-in-law, or as a racing driver (as he was in the *Grand Prix Special*), or as a butler, he always manages to get the audience on his side.

To achieve his appearance, my hair is ruffled up and I wear the Lampwick specs and moustache. A little whitening round the eyes and some shading on the cheeks and forehead make my face look older and more drawn.

As I sit in the make-up chair, I go through my lines, and it is during this time that the character transition takes place. There is nothing profound about this; fortunately I have always been able to slip from one character to another without enormous con-centration. But this ability comes about through long familiarity with the characters — imagine living and working alongside the same people over a period of, say, ten years. You'd get to know their every mannerism, every twitch. And that's how it is with my characters. As I watch myself in the mirror being physically transformed into Lampwick, and hear his lines, there I am—automatically Lampwick.

We all look in the mirror from time to time to check that the signs of growing old are not yet appearing. Most people have the same attitude towards ageing as they do towards accidents—it's some-thing that only happens to other people. And yet all the while there is that sneaking fear . . . Maybe that's why Lampwick is funny to most people—it's a way of laughing off one's fears about the inevitability of old age. And Lampwick represents that will to live and stubborn refusal to submit to the limitations of old age which is the bravest way to cope with this fact of life. I know so many people who, though only in their forties, are older than Lampwick. He and his like are priceless. Their vitality survives all the hardship and afflictions of their lives; like seasoned timbers they are not diminished by age.

I, too, look in the mirror for signs of approaching age, and refuse to believe them when I see them. But in Lampwick, like some ghostly prediction, I have seen myself in years to come. It is not such a very bad prospect.

SCENE: The sitting-room of the Lampwick household. Lily is sitting on the settee placidly knitting. Ernie, her husband, is at the other end of the settee reading a newspaper. Propped against the wall is a large, embroidered British Legion banner. The pleasant domestic peace is suddenly shattered by a blast on a cracked bugle and the sound of tramping feet from upstairs. An ancient gramophone starts to blare forth an old rendering of 'Mademoiselle from Armentiers'. Ernie screws up his paper and glares up at the ceiling.

ERNIE   Lily, I'm asking you—how much longer is this going on?

LILY   How much longer is what going on?

ERNIE   This flaming row. I've lived through the retreat from Mons four times this week already.

LILY   Now don't go on about it, Ernie. You know what Dad's like when it's coming up to his big day.

ERNIE   He's senile, that's what he is. He's in his dotage. They're all potty, marching up and down like a bunch of ruddy kids.

LILY   That is no way to talk about the British Legion. They're a fine bunch of men.

ERNIE   It's like living through an episode of 'All Our Yesterdays' in this house. What's that flag doing there cluttering up the place?

LILY   That's Dad's banner. You know he always carries the banner.

ERNIE   He's a proper little Sister Hannah.

(We hear the sound of the bugle approaching and footsteps descending the stairs. The door bursts open and Dick, as Lampwick, marches in. He is wearing a bowler hat, his best blue suit with wing collar and has campaign medals of the '14-'18 war pinned across his chest. He is wearing a leather sling of the type used for supporting the colours)

LAMPWICK   Lef', right, lef', right . . . halt. Left turn . . . dismiss! *(He obeys his own commands and falls out smartly, putting his bugle down on the table)*

ERNIE   *(disgustedly)* Oh, my gawd! What do you think you're playing at?

LAMPWICK   You shut your face when you're talking to an Old Contemptible.

ERNIE   That's a good word for you.

LAMPWICK   I never saw you in the trenches.

ERNIE   I tried to lie about my age but my nappies fell down.

LILY   Now, stop it, you two.

LAMPWICK   Well, he's got no room to talk. If they'd handed out white feathers in the last lot he'd have looked like a flaming Leghorn chicken.

ERNIE   *(rising and wagging his finger at Lampwick)* That's a lie. I had a very good war record.

LAMPWICK   Yes, I've heard it. Vera Lynn singing 'We'll Meet Again'.

LILY   *(wearily)* Here we go again. 'When I was in the RAF—good old Bomber Command—'

ERNIE   When I was in the RAF—good old Bomber Command, I helped to blow up half the German army.

LAMPWICK   The only thing you ever blew up was the tyres of the Officers' bicycles.

ERNIE   At least I don't go around wearing a lot of phony medals.

64

LAMPWICK	*(furious)* What do you mean, phony medals?
ERNIE	*(prodding Lampwick's chest and raising his voice)* That one there! How long have you had the Order of St Petersburg?
LAMPWICK	*(prodding him back and raising his voice higher)* Ever since I give two tins of corned beef for it.
LILY	Will you shut up, the pair of you?
ERNIE	My gawd, talk about home sweet home. There's no living with him.
LAMPWICK	*(pathetically)* That's right, that's right. Have a go at a poor defenceless old man on his day of glory.
ERNIE	Glory? What are you talking about? You march down the road carrying that silly flag for four hundred yards and straight into the pub. Ten minutes' marching and four hours' boozing—that's your day of glory.
LAMPWICK	*(staring at him, his jaw working)* That . . . silly flag, as you call it, is the banner of the Starch Green branch of the British Legion. And me, Lance Bombadier James Maynard Kitchener Lampwick, being the oldest serving member, has the honour of carrying the banner.
ERNIE .	*(in disgust)* Oh, do what you like with it.
LAMPWICK	If I did what I liked with it, you'd find yourself in the bedroom without having to walk upstairs.

(There is a ring at the doorbell)

LILY	Oh, I wonder who that is? *(She rises and goes out)*
ERNIE	Probably the War Minister come to ask him if it's all right to start another one.
LAMPWICK	*(shaping up to Ernie)* I don't need his permission to have a go at you. *(He swings at Ernie's chin and misses by a couple of feet)*
LILY	*(re-entering)* It's Mr Chapel and Mr Weston for you, Dad.

(Two middle-aged men in blue suits, bowlers and medals enter. They are followed by a very old and decrepit man, similarly dressed, who effaces himself against the wall)

LAMPWICK	Hullo, Sid, hullo, Bert.
SID	'Morning, James.
LAMPWICK	Come about the parade, have you?
SID	*(uncomfortably)* Er, yes, in a way. There's going to be a slight change in the arrangements.
LAMPWICK	Oh yeah.
BERT	You know the branch rule about the standard bearer?
LAMPWICK	I certainly do. The oldest member carries the banner. And a very good and fair rule it is, too.

65

SID   Oh, well, good. We're very pleased you think so, because we'd like you to meet Mr Whitty. *(He indicates the old man, who comes forward and joins the group)*

LAMPWICK   *(looking at the old man suspiciously)* Who's he, then?

SID   He's just . . . joined our branch.

LAMPWICK   *(beginning to grasp the implications and staring at Sid and Bert)* Eh? What . . . are you trying to say?

SID   Well, he's older than you—so . . . he carries the banner.

(There is a dead silence while Lampwick stares at them in disbelief. His eyes bulge and he clutches at his collar and staggers about gasping for breath. Lily rushes to him and steers him to the settee)

LILY   Now see what you've done to him. *(She hastily loosens his collar)*

ERNIE   Yes, I reckon that's disgusting. He's carried your rotten old flag for you for years and now you drop him for some Johnny-come-lately.

LAMPWICK   *(pointing a trembling finger at Whitty)* Get him out of here. Get him out.

BERT   Jim, I know how you feel, but rules are rules.

LAMPWICK   You're not taking the Legion's banner from me. I was a founder member.

BERT   Come on, Jim—hand it over.

(He places a fist on the staff of the banner. Lampwick replies by putting his hand above Bert's—who counters with a hand above Lampwick's. Their hands rapidly climb up the banner until Lampwick is on tip-toe)

BERT   *(exasperated)* Now look here, this is getting us nowhere. *(To Sid)* See what you can do.

SID   Right. That's enough of that. Lance Bombadier Lampwick, since I out-rank you, I am giving you a direct order. Hand over that banner!

LAMPWICK   *(defiantly)* No!

SID   *(sergeant major voice)* Do as you're told or I'll have that stripe off your arm!

(They glare at each other eyeball to eyeball. Lampwick's resistance suddenly crumbles. Slowly he allows Sid to take the banner from him. He turns away)

LAMPWICK   *(brokenly)* That's it, then. There's nothing left. I'm not much longer for this world. And when I'm called by that Supreme Commander in the sky . . . *(we hear the faint, distant strains of the last post)* and he'll see me on parade and he'll say, 'Well, Jim, did you carry the banner till the end?' And I'll say, 'No, sir, they took it off me.' And he'll say, 'Oh, Jim, why was that, son?' And I'll say *(his voice slowly rises)* 'Because some dirty,

	lying, mangy old bag of bones came in at the last minute and worked me a flanker. That's bloody why!'
LILY	*(shocked)* Dad!
ERNIE	*(admiringly)* He's marvellous, isn't he? Next week 'The Death of Nelson'.
SID	All right, Mr Whitty, come here. *(There is no response from Whitty)* Bert, give him a nudge, will you.
BERT	Let's try it for size. *(He raises the banner and suddenly realises that Whitty is not wearing a pouch)* Where's the pouch?
LAMPWICK	I've got it and you're not having it because it's mine.
LILY	Dad, how can the poor old soul carry the banner without the pouch?
LAMPWICK	Let him stick it down his flies. At his time of life he's got nothing to lose.
ERNIE	*(admiringly)* He's marvellous, isn't he?
LILY	Be quiet, Ernie, you're no help at all. Come on, Dad, hand it over.

(She takes the sling from round Lampwick's shoulders and hands it to Bert who puts it on Whitty)

SID	Right, now then.

(He inserts the end of the staff into the pouch. Whitty grasps the banner with both hands. Very slowly, his knees begin to buckle. He sinks to the floor, first on his knees and then flat on his face. Lampwick falls about laughing)

LAMPWICK	Blimey, if he's going to carry the banner, who's going to carry *him*?
SID	Well, Jim, looks as though we'll have to call on your good offices once again. *(He offers Lampwick the banner)* You carry the banner.
LILY	Well, thank goodness that's settled.
SID	Right. See you on parade at twelve o'clock. Come on, Mr Whitty.

(Sid and Bert exit supporting Whitty between them. Lily goes to see them out. Lampwick tucks the banner under his arm and laughs smugly)

ERNIE	Well, I must say, there's no fool like an old fool.
LAMPWICK	To which I reply—if at first you don't succeed . . . *(He walks to the door and as he goes through he knocks the flag on the top of the doorway. The flag pole breaks in half)*
ERNIE	And I give you—he who laughs last laughs longest.

INTERVIEWER *Excuse me, sir . . .*
BOVVER BOY   *Yer?*
INTERVIEWER *Tell me, have you ever had a premonition?*
BOVVER BOY   *A what?*
INTERVIEWER *Have you ever had a strange feeling that something was going to go wrong?*
BOVVER BOY   *Oh, yer. I had it last year. I'd just knocked off this big black motor, see . . . and as soon as I got in it I had this strange feeling that something was going to go wrong.*
INTERVIEWER *And why do you think that was?*
BOVVER BOY   *There was two coppers sitting in the back seat.*

THE BOVVER BOY

The Bovver Boy

The Bovver Boy

On the face of it, there isn't much to be said in favour of this uncouth youth with his crew cut, bovver boots and tendency to express himself by kicking savagely at the nearest object. However, he seems popular enough, and I've often been asked to demonstrate his kick, just as I'm asked to do the Old Colonel's gammy leg, which has to be steered round corners, or Mandy's punchline, or Lampwick's strangulated struggle to get his words out.

I know that people mean well, but they often seem to expect me to turn up in one of my character guises when I'm invited to open a fête or attend a function! I sometimes think that poor Dick Emery is in danger of disappearing altogether—and it is important to me to retain some form of identity for myself, if only so that my characters don't get inflated ideas of their own importance.

The Bovver Boy replaced an earlier creation who went out of fashion, the Teddy Boy, and was created during the *Grand Prix Special* programme I mentioned earlier. Originally, we had intended to experiment with candid camera work, and film me from a hidden lens as I wandered about Cambridge market in my various character guises—and this is how the Bovver Boy first met the cameras. As Lampwick, I tried begging a cup of tea—and succeeded in getting one! So now I know that whatever else befalls me, I shan't go short of the price of a cuppa!

As Mandy, I was outrageous. I stood in the middle of a busy

street and touted for a lift. This provoked various reactions from passing motorists—mostly disbelief at the sauce of this hideous apparition. And none of them stopped. With perfect British aplomb they pretended not to see what was patently there—a coarse woman literally flaunting herself in order to get attention. Unfortunately the session was called off for technical reasons, but it was certainly a memorable day's filming.

I seem to have strayed away from the Bovver Boy—poor fellow, no wonder he kicks up. The only way he and his kind can draw to themselves the attention which they crave in the face of indifference and rejection, is to resort to a group identity and commit petty acts of senseless violence. And the press and media play a major part in encouraging them by satisfying their desire to be noticed and reporting the extent of the damage and trouble caused. At last, the Bovver Boys have produced a reaction from an otherwise pre-occupied society. And, seeing that they can thus focus attention on themselves and become important, they cause more trouble, and the press continues to report it. Perhaps if there was less coverage of this kind of vandalism in the papers, there would be less trouble from the vandals. As it is, I sometimes wonder if leading Bovver Boys have press cutting agencies!

We all have deep within us a natural streak of aggression, but in most of us it is channelled into peaceful directions, or at least, controlled. But in the absence of any interest or aim in life, and with the probability of bad parental example, the Bovver Boy's aggression has been allowed to develop. And I feel sorry for him.

When I portray him on the screen, I am not making fun of his aimlessness or ignorance. I feel that many like him are in a hopeless situation. So he talks about violence and swings his boot, feeling left out and frustrated, and mad at everyone who seemingly has more to do and enjoy in life. He doesn't mean half what he says, but it makes him feel bigger to act tough.

If you find him funny, I wonder if it's because you recognize his feelings in yourself, and can sympathize while laughing at his exaggerated mannerism?

INTERVIEWER   *Excuse me, sir.*
BOVVER BOY   *Yer?*
INTERVIEWER   *Is there anything in life that you feel you've missed?*
BOVVER BOY   *Yer. I never learnt to drive.*
INTERVIEWER   *That's no great handicap, not being able to drive.*
BOVVER BOY   *It is when you're a car thief!*

SCENE: Interior of the Principal's office at the Theodore Cobbold Foundling Home. The room is furnished with a desk and chairs for visitors. There is a door on the left. The Principal, Mr Crowthorne, is seated behind his desk engaged in some paperwork. There is a knock at the door.

PRINCIPAL   Come in.

(The door opens to admit a girl carrying a baby)

GIRL   Excuse me, Mr Crowthorne. Mr and Mrs Shipley are here to see you.
PRINCIPAL   Oh, yes. Ask them to come in, will you?

(A tall, thin man in his early thirties enters, followed by his attractive wife Amanda)

PRINCIPAL   *(with outstretched hand)* Mr Shipley, how are you?

(Amanda pauses and looks at the baby)

AMANDA   Isn't he gorgeous? *(She sighs mistily. The girl smiles and exits)*
PRINCIPAL   Mrs Shipley . . . do come and sit down, both of you.
PETER   *(eagerly)* Well, Mr Crowthorne — any news?
PRINCIPAL   I hate to disappoint you both but I'm afraid we have no babies available for adoption at the moment.
PETER   Oh, what a damn shame.·
AMANDA   Yes, we had so set our hearts on having a little brother for our Timothy.
PRINCIPAL   I'm sorry. Perhaps you could try some other . . .
AMANDA   *(woefully)* We've tried everywhere.
PETER   There, there, darling. At least it proves there are no unwanted babies in the world, thank goodness.
AMANDA   Are you absolutely certain, Mr Crowthorne, that you can't help us?
PRINCIPAL   *(dubiously)* Well . . . *(He opens a card index on his desk and starts to riffle through it)* There is one . . . but not a baby, I'm afraid.
PETER   Oh, we don't mind a toddler, do we, Amanda?
AMANDA   No, no, not a bit. We'd love one.
PETER   He could teach little Timothy to walk.
PRINCIPAL   Yes . . . he could. He could certainly do that. Look, the best thing would be for you to meet each other and see how you get on.
AMANDA   Yes! Yes, please. Where is the little darling?
PRINCIPAL   I'll have him brought up. *(He exits)*
AMANDA   Oh, Peter, how marvellous. There's still a chance.
PETER   Yes. I'd hate to see that little nursery go to waste, with the piggywigs and bunnies on the wall.
AMANDA   Can't you just imagine the two of them in the bath together — playing with their rubber ducks?

(The door is kicked open with a crash. Framed in the doorway is Dick, dressed as the Bovver Boy, with the big boots, braces and cropped hair. He flings wide his arms)

76

BOVVER BOY   Where's my new Mummy and Daddy?

(Amanda and Peter recoil in horror)

PETER   My God!

AMANDA   Oh, no!

(The Bovver Boy advances into the room)

BOVVER BOY   Hullo, Dad. *(He looks at Amanda and his eyes widen)* And you're going to be my Mummy. Cor! Giss a kiss. *(He grabs Amanda and bends her backwards in a passionate embrace)*

PETER   All right . . . that's enough . . . *(his voice rises)* leave her alone! *(He shouts and pounds the Bovver Boy's back)* Get off her!

(The Bovver Boy releases Amanda, turns and looks accusingly at Peter)

BOVVER BOY   You hit me. That's a nice thing for a Daddy to do when his little boy's having a cuddle with Mummy.

PETER   I'm sorry. I didn't mean to strike you . . . but this is all a mistake.

BOVVER BOY   Oh. And Mr Crowthorne said you'd be pleased to see me.

PETER   *(aghast)* You mean . . . you're the . . . he thinks . . .

AMANDA   Peter, I'm going to be sick.

BOVVER BOY   I promise to be a good little boy.

PETER   But you're not, dammit! You're not a little boy. How old are you?

BOVVER BOY   Would you believe twelve?

PETER   *(vehemently)* No, I wouldn't.

BOVVER BOY   All right, then—thirty-three.

PETER   Good God, you're older than I am.

BOVVER BOY   Perhaps I'd better adopt you.

PETER   No. No. The whole thing is . . . grotesque.

BOVVER BOY   Don't send me away. You've got to take me, otherwise there'll be beatings and kickings and horrible things like that.

PETER   Are you trying to tell us that Mr Crowthorne does that to you?

BOVVER BOY   No. I do that to Mr Crowthorne.

PETER   Look, now look—there's nothing personal about this. But you see, we're looking for a lovable, adorable little child . . . not a horror like you . . . *(He claps his hand over his mouth)* Oh, I'm sorry. I didn't mean that.

BOVVER BOY   *(pathetic)* That's nice, isn't it.

AMANDA   Peter, that was a dreadful thing to say. *(She nervously approaches the Bovver Boy, who, with head bowed, is starting to snivel)* Please, don't take any notice

77

	of what my husband said. I don't think you're a . . . a . . . horror. In fact, you're quite . . . attractive.
BOVVER BOY	Do you really mean that?
AMANDA	Yes, I do.
BOVVER BOY	Giss a kiss, then. *(Once again he grabs her as Peter hovers about ineffectually)*
PETER	Put her down, come on . . . stop that, d'you hear me? That's enough! Let go. Let go! *(He prises the Bovver Boy and Amanda apart)*
BOVVER BOY	You don't know what it's like to be starved of affection. I'm looking for love.
PETER	I know what you're looking for—and you won't find it in my home!
AMANDA	You see, we've got a little boy—Timothy—and he needs a playmate.
BOVVER BOY	I'd play with him. I'd teach him to play 'Cops and Robbers', like I do. With real coppers. I could take him to football and show him how to play trains.
PETER	You like to play trains?
BOVVER BOY	*With* trains—on the way to the match. He could do the seats while I do the light bulbs.
AMANDA	What a ghastly thought!
BOVVER BOY	How about writing? I could teach him to write. *(He produces an aerosol paint can from his pocket and starts writing on the wall of the office)* S P U R S Up the Blues. I could teach him poems. I know some good ones. 'If I had a donkey, I'd give him lots of grass, and if he wouldn't eat it, I'd—
PETER	Stop it, stop it. Come on, darling, we're going. *(He shakes a finger at the Bovver Boy)* Don't you dare follow us home—don't you dare!

(They rush out, slamming the door)

| BOVVER BOY | Whatsamatter? Is it something I said? *(He thrusts his hands in his pockets miserably)* I dunno. Why is it nobody loves me? |

(He aims a casual kick at the desk. The leg of it falls off. The door opens and Crowthorne enters)

| PRINCIPAL | You've done it again, haven't you! I'll never get rid of you   and do you know why? Because you're a monster. Well, you've had your last chance, Screwsby, your last chance! |

(The door opens. Framed in the doorway is an enormous, late-middle-aged man, dressed in every detail the same as the Bovver Boy. A tough-looking woman hovers at his shoulder)

| MAN | Excuse me, is this where you come to adopt a kid? |

78

PRINCIPAL	Go away, we haven't got any.
MAN	*(indicating the Bovver Boy)* What about him?
PRINCIPAL	. . . Him?
MAN	Yer. He's a little beauty. Mum, look at his lovely head.
WOMAN	Cor, isn't he gorgeous.

(The Bovver Boy moves towards them, uncertainly)

BOVVER BOY	Mum? Dad?
MAN	Of course.

(The woman hugs the Bovver Boy. The man looks over his shoulder at the writing on the wall)

MAN	Here, who wrote that up there?
BOVVER BOY	*(brightly)* I did, Dad.
MAN	And you done it lovely. *(He belts the Bovver Boy round the ear)* Only don't do it again—we're Chelsea supporters.
BOVVER BOY	Up Chelsea!
MAN	Come on, son.

(With their arms round each other, the three exit)

(The interviewer approaches the Bovver Boy, who is leaning against a wall and has a pram on the end of a piece of string. He keeps pushing the pram away and hauling it back on the rope)

INTERVIEWER   *Excuse me, sir . . .*
BOVVER BOY   *Yer?*
INTERVIEWER   *Er . . . what are you doing with that pram?*
BOVVER BOY   *Taking my sister's baby for a walk.*
INTERVIEWER   *Oh. Well, I wonder if you'd mind answering a question. We all have bad days in our lives—can you think of one in particular?*
BOVVER BOY   *Yer, I can think of a shocking awful day.*
INTERVIEWER   *Yes?*
BOVVER BOY   *Some villain set light to the local nick and all the coppers came running out with their backsides on fire.*
INTERVIEWER   *Terrible! And when did that happen?*
BOVVER BOY   *Termorrer.*

CLARENCE

Clarence

Clarence

Clarence is another popular character in my collection. Wearing outrageous clothes which would frighten all but the bravest of spirits, he has a one-track mind and yet is completely harmless and his natural gaiety and optimism are quite infectious.

He is a product of the many variety shows I have worked in over the years. Drag and camp acts are nothing new—thirty years ago there were plenty of show business characters who would sidle up to you and simper 'Hullo, dear, how are *you*?' in tones very reminiscent of Clarence's. When variety was very popular, every production had several Clarences in the chorus line. And always they were gentle and charming, with a sense of humour and a professionalism on stage which made them a pleasure to work with.

Clarence has undergone probably the biggest change of any of my characters. When he began life, male fashions were far more subdued than they are today, and so his effeminacy had to be shown through his make-up; also he wore a wig of short, blond, swept-back hair. However, men started to wear brighter and more adventurous clothes, and Clarence found that he was beginning to be outdone. In order to stand out, he had to become fashion-conscious. But these days it is difficult to keep him ahead of fashion—what Clarence wears one week, the trendies are wearing the next, or so it seems! Now, with more emphasis on his clothes, he needs less make-up and no wig at all.

83

There was a time when I would get upset because people confused me with my characters, and assumed that because Clarence is a homosexual, so I must be also. But nowadays it doesn't worry me. For some reason, many comedians have a built-in element of effeminacy in their acts. Chaplin had it, so did Sid Fields—even Jack Benny has it. And most comedians recognize that by becoming a little precious they can raise an instant laugh—a useful ploy in cabaret, for instance, when you're faced with an unresponsive audience staring blankly at you across their plates of steak and chips. Why the suggestion of homosexuality should be funny is an imponderable—perhaps our laughter is a defence, a reaction against hidden fears about our own innermost tendencies.

INTERVIEWER	*Excuse me, sir.*
CLARENCE	*Oh, hullo Honky Tonks, how are you? Nice to see.*
INTERVIEWER	*I'm asking questions about class distinction.*
CLARENCE	*Oh, yes.*
INTERVIEWER	*Do you believe there's an 'us' and a 'them'?*
CLARENCE	*Well, it doesn't bother me, really—I'm one of those!*

THE SPORTING GENT

The Sporting Gent

The Sporting Gent

Never buy a motor car from this man. Or anything else, for that matter, because he is the genuine British cad. He is interested in your wallet, possibly your wife, but definitely not in you—unless it's your round, that is!

He is identified by his loudly checked jacket, jaunty bow-tie, flat cap and thin, well-trimmed moustache, and is usually to be found in the smarter bars, drinking shorts—which he never buys himself, if he can help it. He boasts about his club, but is careful not to mention which one it is (it's probably the local Christmas Club!), and regales all and sundry with smutty jokes and jests about 'the wife'. His car is probably an open model of some sort, certainly not new. And, being the sporting type, he'll drive it with the hood down until the frost makes the soft roof too stiff to unroll.

I like to think he's the outcast black sheep of a well-to-do family. The kind of tweeds his father wore have been replaced with a louder pattern in accordance with his flashy taste. His former huntin', shootin' and fishin' activities have been replaced by the compara- tively cheaper pursuit of the ladies. To compensate for his loss of station, the Sporting Gent has to overstate everything. He seems to be the life and soul of the party with his jokes and jaunty sports car, but he probably goes back to an untidy, characterless flat, where he sits alone still sporting his brave bow-tie and tweeds. Keeping up appearances is important to us all: to this man they have to compensate for everything else.

The Sporting Gent probably sells cars for a living, capitalizing on his easy line of chat and preying on the gullible — he could talk an aged widow with three spaniels into buying a Fiat 500. However, the man I based him on was an RAF Entertainment Officer I encountered during the war. I was performing in one of Ralph Reader's Gang Shows—in peacetime they were and still are, of course, performed by Scouts—and we had been posted to Normandy some few days after D-Day to entertain the troops and keep up morale. When we landed, shaky and glad to be on terra firma again, this chap—a real RAF type—came up and asked with concern where the girls were. To be asking about girls, when as he spoke we could hear Caen being bombed to pieces! When we told him that we played the girls' roles as well, he gave that 'Ha ha ha' which has become the Sporting Gent's familiar guffaw.

This type is usually so preoccupied with himself that he is completely insensitive to the feeling and well-being of others. I remember we had completed a fortnight's tour, which entailed sometimes two shows a day, with each of us playing every conceivable part, and erecting and dismantling the stage before and after every performance. We were utterly exhausted. Eventually the RAF Entertainment Officer noticed us sitting around listlessly, and asked why. He was amazed when we pointed out how tired we were. 'Good Lord—you all looked so happy and cheerful,' he said. It had never occurred to him that we might actually be working very hard to keep up the cheerful appearance!

I expect I started using him as material on those make-shift stages for the benefit of the troops, though the character has developed over the years as I've met more like him and understood more of their mentality. Certainly, I used him often in my radio appearances, such as *Variety Bandbox*, where his 'Ha ha ha' chortle echoed over the air like some ghost of that original Entertainment Officer. He was, sadly, killed during the war.

The Sporting Gent has his own particular sceptical frown, and I turn in the edges of my mouth slightly in order to change the shape of my chin so that I look different from the Traffic Warden, for instance, or any other character who needs little make-up. And of course, this Sporting Gent has that annoying habit of standing with his hands deep in his pockets, jingling his coins while he speaks.

INTERVIEWER	*Pardon me, sir . . .*
SPORTING GENT	*Yes, old boy?*
INTERVIEWER	*Do you believe in being a good neighbour?*
SPORTING GENT	*I most certainly do, old chap. Take the other evening—my neighbour's little pussy got stuck up on our roof. I climbed up to get it down and fell through straight into the au pair's bed.*
INTERVIEWER	*That's unbelievable!*
SPORTING GENT	*That's exactly what my wife's solicitor said.* (To glamorous blonde on his arm) *Didn't he, Ingrid? Come on, darling.*

INTERVIEWER	*Excuse me, sir . . .*
SPORTING GENT	*Yes, old boy?*
INTERVIEWER	*I'm asking about family relationships.*
SPORTING GENT	*Don't mention family to me. Mine has just cost me a bomb.*
INTERVIEWER	*Really?*
SPORTING GENT	*I've just paid two hundred quid to some idiot to have my family history traced.*
INTERVIEWER	*That's very interesting.*
SPORTING GENT	*What? Cost me another three hundred to have it hushed up!*

BRIEF ENCOUNTER

SCENE: An empty first-class railway compartment with the corridor upstage. Peter, a man in his early forties, appears in the corridor. He is carrying a small suitcase. He is followed by Helen, an attractive woman in her early thirties. She also carries a suitcase. Peter opens the door.

PETER   Here we are, darling.

(He puts their suitcases up on the rack, then closes the door. They both sit on the left-hand side of the compartment, Peter upstage of Helen. He grabs her hand and tries to kiss her. She turns her face away)

HELEN   Please, Peter, you must give me time to adjust. After all, it's not every day I run away from my husband.

PETER   I know, old girl. I feel a bit shaky myself. I've never left the wife before.

HELEN   But it had to be, didn't it, darling? It was purgatory living next door to you and being unable to touch you.

PETER   It was worse for me, seeing your underwear on the line every Monday morning.

HELEN   We must take our happiness while we can. The only thing that worries me is Clive. I know he'll be broken up. I only hope he doesn't . . . do something silly.

PETER   There, there, darling.

(Dick appears in the corridor. He is dressed as Clive, the sporting gent, in a rather loud hacking jacket. He is followed by Angela, another attractive, well-dressed woman. She is carrying two suitcases and a bag of golf clubs. Clive glances into the compartment at the empty seats on the right, and opens the door)

CLIVE   Here we are, sweetheart. Shove 'em up on the rack, old thing. *(He watches Angela struggle with the cases)* Well done.

(They sit on the right-hand side of the compartment, with Clive in the upstage corner seat. They look at each other fondly and hold hands. Peter and Helen stare at them in shocked recognition)

PETER   Angela!

ANGELA   *(turning in horror)* Peter!

HELEN   Clive!

CLIVE   Hell!

PETER   What the devil are you doing with my wife?

CLIVE   And I might ask you the same.

PETER   If you want to know, old man, we're running away together.

CLIVE   You rotten swine.

PETER   Well, what about you and Angela?

CLIVE   I'm a rotten swine, too, I suppose.

PETER   You don't mean that you two . . . ?

ANGELA   I'm leaving you, Peter . . . for Clive.

94

HELEN	Angela, how could you! My best friend!
CLIVE	Huh, that's rich. Sitting there practically seducing her husband.
HELEN	That's different. We love each other.
CLIVE	How long have you two been . . . carrying on?
PETER	Well, if you must know—about six months.
CLIVE	(*triumphantly*) Ha! Gotcher—we've been at it for eight months, haven't we, old girl?
PETER	You rotter! Do you mean to say you two have been . . . *you* know?
CLIVE	Yes.
ANGELA	Certainly not.
CLIVE	Yes, certainly not. Tell you one thing, I'll lay you six to four you two haven't . . . er . . . *you* know.
HELEN	What do you mean?
CLIVE	Well, if I know you, darling, it's either 'Don't be so disgusting' or 'Can't you see I'm reading?'.
PETER	I find this whole thing highly embarrassing. The least you could do is find another compartment.

(*A ticket inspector appears in the corridor*)

CLIVE	I don't see why we should. We're perfectly comfortable here.

(*The inspector opens the door and enters*)

HELEN	You always were a selfish, unreasonable brute.
CLIVE	As a wife, dear, you were a flaming disaster.
PETER	How dare you speak to her like that. When you've lived with my wife for a few months you'll realise that Helen is a perfect treasure.
ANGELA	And she'll find that as a husband you're a perfect bore.

(*The inspector has been watching these exchanges with some interest*)

INSPECTOR	Can I see your tickets, please?
PETER	(*producing two tickets immediately*) Here you are.

(*The inspector clips the tickets and turns to Clive*)

CLIVE	Sorry, old chap, we nearly missed the train. I didn't have time to buy tickets.
INSPECTOR	Where are you going, sir?
CLIVE	Bournemouth.
PETER	You rotten creep, so are we.
HELEN	Not the Cranley Arms?

CLIVE   *(cheerfully)* That's right, old thing. Where we spent our honeymoon. *(Helen bursts into tears. Peter puts an arm round her shoulders)* I'll never forget that night. I want to warn you, old boy, the walls are so thin you have to oil the bedsprings before you start the old nonsense.

PETER   *(savagely)* You unutterable cad.

INSPECTOR   That'll be five pounds ten, sir, please.

CLIVE   *(peering in his wallet)* Oh, lor'. I completely forgot to go to the bank. *(To Helen)* You haven't got a few quid, have you, darling? *(Helen instantly stops crying and falls into her familiar role of wife. She opens her handbag)*

HELEN   I don't think so, dear. No. Peter?

PETER   I'm afraid I'm a bit short myself. Angela?

ANGELA   *(producing notes from her bag)* Here you are, darling.

PETER   Thanks, poppet. *(He hands them to Helen)* Sweetheart?

HELEN   *(handing them to Clive)* Dearest?

CLIVE   Thanks, sweetie. *(He hands them to the inspector)* Here you are, gorgeous . . . I mean . . . inspector.

INSPECTOR   I only hope you're all going to wait till you get to Bournemouth — otherwise I'll draw the blinds. *(He exits, tut-tutting)*

HELEN   *(producing an envelope from her handbag)* I was going to post this to you, Clive. It's my farewell letter.

CLIVE   Oh, that's damn decent of you, old girl. *(He also produces a letter)* I've got one for you. Might as well save a stamp.

ANGELA   *(handing over an envelope)* I've written one to you, too, Peter.

PETER   *(passing a letter to Angela)* Thanks. Here's yours.

CLIVE   Excuse me.

PETER   Excuse me. *(All four sit back, open their letters and start to read. There is silence for several beats. Clive starts to chuckle and then laughs out loud)*

CLIVE   Good lord, so you knew all the time.

HELEN   About what, darling?

CLIVE   About the blonde bit who works at the library.

HELEN   Well, I got rather suspicious when you went to change your books twice a week and always came back with *Marriage for Beginners*.

CLIVE   Damn it all, darling, having lived with you for ten years I had to refresh my memory.

HELEN   *(to Angela)* You see what you've let yourself in for?

ANGELA   Well, you needn't think you're the only other woman in Peter's life.

CLIVE   No. Knowing that blighter, I doubt if you're in the Top Ten.

96

PETER	*(waving his letter angrily at Angela)* What the hell do you mean, I think more of the golf club than I do of you?
ANGELA	Well, so you did. Until I made you give it up.
	(Clive stares at Angela in horror and turns to Peter)
CLIVE	She made you give it up . . . golf? Good God! I'm surprised you didn't leave her years ago.
PETER	Yes. When we moved in next door to you, she took one look at that damn great garden and bang went my weekends.
CLIVE	You poor old chap. Look here, I feel absolutely rotten. I'd no idea you were a brother golfer. I'd never have tried it on with your missus if I'd known.
ANGELA	Clive!
PETER	Apology accepted, old man.
CLIVE	After all, I'm Club Captain this year.
PETER	I say! I'm sorry to have put you in this embarrassing position . . . skipper.
HELEN	Peter!
CLIVE	That's all right, old boy. But I don't want to give those old elephant-trousered bags in the Ladies' Section something else to gnash their false choppers over.
PETER	Oh, right, right! By the way, what's your handicap?
CLIVE	Nine.
ANGELA	Clive?
PETER	Me too.
HELEN	Peter!
CLIVE	Have you ever played Bournemouth? It's a cracking course. Look here, we could have a damn good weekend's golf.
PETER	*(eagerly)* We could borrow some clubs . . .
CLIVE	And stay out at the Golf Club.
HELEN	What about us?
CLIVE	Sorry, old girl. All that late night hanky-panky plays absolute havoc with one's swing. Come on, Peter old boy, let's go and have a drink. *(They go out)* No, the first is a rather long dogleg left. I usually play out to the right . . . *(They disappear. The girls look at each other and burst into loud tears)*

INTERVIEWER	*Excuse me, sir.*
SPORTING GENT	*Oh, yes?*
INTERVIEWER	*May I ask you a question? What do you think of the working class?*
SPORTING GENT	*Oh ghastly. Absolute villains. D'you know, about a couple of weeks ago my chauffeur pinched my Rolls? Haven't seen hide nor hair of it since.*
INTERVIEWER	*Oh, but haven't you tried to recover it?*
SPORTING GENT	*Oh, certainly not, no—the Missus was in the back!* (To glamorous dollybird on his arm) *Come on, darling.*

COLLEGE

College

College

Tramp characters have always had a strong appeal for comedians because they offer such wide scope for comedy situations and characterization, and College is far from being the first tramp I have ever played. I have been using him, though, as a consistent character, for about three years now, and he is just reaching that interesting stage where, having established himself, he can develop and grow into an even more important member of my troupe. This is an exciting period in his development, because I can now motivate him from within the framework of his own established character rather than imposing reasons why he should act in certain ways. He is beginning to come alive and have a personality of his own. The scriptwriters have helped enormously in the development of College.

His very name suggests that he has had some kind of education, and he seems to have enjoyed a rather different background from the usual down-and-out tramp. The humour of the situation comes from the difference between College's actual station in life, and his refusal to acknowledge his reduced circumstances. He remains a gentleman with cultural pretensions while slumming it with his friend Droopy. He retains the vestiges of his former life, with his old school tie, battered bowler hat and crumpled buttonhole. And if he met a fellow 'old boy' from his school taking a stroll through the park where College sleeps every night, he would act as though their stations in life were equal, and his misfortunes would become even less real to him.

The audience likes him for his refusal to kotow to the bureaucrats of this world with whom he comes into contact, and because he is a kind of anti-establishment figure who makes chaos out of order.

I hope that eventually we will be able to develop the pathetic side of his character, too, so that the audience's laughter at his cunning and the devious ways in which he contrives to come off best in spite of everything, will be mixed with compassion and understanding. He already has the goodwill of the audience— after all, everyone can afford to feel sympathy for this down-and-out with the indomitable spirit. He is, in fact, Chaplin's 'little man' struggling to retain his dignity in the face of heavy odds and the massed authority of the various powers-that-be.

SCENE: A typical small branch of the Ministry of Employment and Social Security. There is a counter on the right and a door on the left, an electric fire against the wall downstage of the door, and chairs round the walls.

(The door opens and Dick, as College, pokes his head in)

COLLEGE   Ah. Here we are. *(He enters and holds the door open)* Come on in, Droopy, old son.

(College is dressed in his usual battered finery and wields an ancient umbrella. Droopy wears a ragged overcoat and a stained trilby. He carries a large paper carrier bag. He looks around, open-mouthed)

DROOPY   Where are we, College?

COLLEGE   *(closing the door)* The Min of Emp and Soc Sec, old boy.

DROOPY   The what?

COLLEGE   The Ministry of Employment and Social Security—the old Labour Exchange.

(Droopy makes a bolt for the door. College restrains him with a hand on the shoulder)

COLLEGE   My goodness, that word has a remarkable effect on you.

DROOPY   I don't want a job, College.

COLLEGE   Good Lord, neither do I, old son. Perish the thought.

DROOPY   Then what are we doing here?

COLLEGE   From past experience I can assure you this is the warmest place in this godforsaken town. Now, let us take advantage of the amenities. *(He places two chairs in front of the electric fire)* Do take a seat, old lad.

DROOPY   That's nice of you, College. Ta. All right to take the boots off?

COLLEGE   Steam away, old son.

(Droopy kicks off his boots and stretches his toes to the fire as College puts the kettle on top of it. He seats himself, takes off his bowler, wipes it with his sleeve and hangs it on the back of another chair on which he puts his feet. He takes out a tobacco tin, sorts out a decent cigar butt and lights it)

COLLEGE   Comfy, old chap?

DROOPY   Home from home, College, that's what this is. Home from home.

COLLEGE   Um. I say, those old grey socks of yours are drying out nicely.

DROOPY   I'm not wearing any socks.

COLLEGE   I stand corrected. Your old grey feet are drying out nicely. *(He stretches over to a nearby small table and takes one of a pile of leaflets)* I say, this is damned interesting. Do you know, if you were pregnant, we'd be on a stone bonker twenty quid and six months' free orange juice.

DROOPY   But I'm not.

COLLEGE   If you were, old boy, I'd have you on 'Opportunity Knocks' like a shot.

106

DROOPY   *(looking round at the vacant counter)* Here, I suppose it's all right, us being here?

COLLEGE   All right? Of course it's all right. It's people like us who keep places like this open. They'll be delighted to see us.

(A man in a blue serge suit appears behind the counter. He is carrying a small metal tray with a cup of tea and a plate of sandwiches. He plonks the tray down on the counter and glares at College and Droopy)

MAN   What the hell do you think you're doing?

(Droopy leaps to his feet and grabs his boots. College remains languidly seated)

COLLEGE   Stand fast, Droopy, old fellow.

MAN   Oh, it's you again, is it? Clear off, go on. Out. *(He indicates Droopy)* And take that thing with you.

COLLEGE   *(rising and putting on his bowler)* Have a care, my good man. A word in the Minister's ear and you could find yourself on *this* side of the counter.

MAN   Look, I remember you from last time. Came in here claiming to be an out-of-work brain surgeon and bouncing us for twenty quid to get your tools out of pawn! Go on, hop it! And get all that rubbish out of here.

COLLEGE   My dear minion, I am not here on my own behalf but in loco parentis, as you might say, for my colleague, who finds himself in reduced circumstances.

MAN   *(through clenched teeth)* Is he applying for a job?

COLLEGE   Yes, he is.

(Without looking he grabs Droopy, who has started to bolt)

MAN   *(reaching for a form)* All right, then. *(He prepares to write)* What are his qualifications?

COLLEGE   First of all he is the professional, world champion left-handed Mah Jong player. *(The man sighs heavily)* He also spent seven years in the mystic east studying under the Maharajah of Cooch Bawani and achieved the D.A.E.W.

MAN   I know I'm going to regret this but what does that stand for?

COLLEGE   Diploma in Advanced Elephant Washing. *(He picks up the cup of tea from the counter and sips it)*

MAN   *(heavily)* That happens to be my cup you're drinking out of.

COLLEGE   I do beg your pardon. *(He pours tea into the saucer and drinks)*

MAN   *(sarcastically)* You wouldn't fancy a sandwich, I suppose?

COLLEGE   How terribly kind. *(He takes a sandwich from the plate and bites into it. The man stares at him in disbelief. College smacks his lips discerningly)* Um. I think you might mention to the wife that bloater paste is hardly the fodder for an up-and-coming executive.

MAN   You've got the sauce of the devil, you have. Now, get out of it!

COLLEGE   What about my associate? He is still without employment.

MAN   And he's going to stay that way.

DROOPY   Thank gawd for that.

COLLEGE   Very well. Since you can be of no assistance, we shall leave.

MAN   Good riddance.

COLLEGE   Come, Droopy. *(He makes a false exit)* Oh, by the way, can you direct me to the department that deals with grants?

MAN   *(holding his head)* Oh, my gawd! I knew it was too good to be true. I deal with that.

COLLEGE   Ah. Good morning. *(He raises his bowler politely)* I wonder if you could assist me? My colleague here wishes to make an application for a grant.

MAN   What for?

COLLEGE   A bathroom.

MAN   A what?

DROOPY   A what?

COLLEGE   A bathroom. I understand that government funds are available for such a purpose.

MAN   Well, yes, they are.

COLLEGE   Good. Round about a thousand will do. We'll take it in cash.

MAN   Hang on a minute. Those baths are for people who need them.

COLLEGE   Have you ever seen anyone who needs a bath more than he does?

MAN   Stop wasting my time.

COLLEGE   I demand compensation for his chickens.

MAN   What chickens?

COLLEGE   Struck down by swine fever.

MAN   That only affects pigs.

COLLEGE   And his pigs.

MAN   Try again.

COLLEGE   What about his free school dinners?

MAN   Hop it!

COLLEGE   He offers his services for artificial insemination.

MAN   Look, there is no way you can get a farthing out of me.

COLLEGE   Very well, you leave me no alternative. *(He picks up a bottle of ink from the counter and throws it in Droopy's face)*

DROOPY   *(aghast)* What did you do that for?

108

COLLEGE	*(to the man)* Yes, what *did* you do that for?
MAN	Who, me?
COLLEGE	Why did you commit that unprovoked attack on my friend? A man who has staggered fifty miles in his bare feet looking for honest employment.
MAN	I never touched him!

(College picks up the sandwich plate)

COLLEGE	Put down that plate, sir. *(He smashes it over Droopy's head)* My God, is there no limit to your cruelty? *(He staggers theatrically towards the door)* I must summon public assistance to avert this slaughter of the innocents.
MAN	*(panicking)* No, no! Wait, wait!

(College moves back towards the counter)

MAN	*(raising a clenched fist in impotent fury)* You . . . you . . .!
COLLEGE	You're at it again. Curb your anger, sir.
MAN	All right. I'll tell you what I'll do. I'm empowered to give you a shilling a mile to go and be interviewed for a job. *(He puts notes on the counter)* Here's three quid. Go and apply for one thirty miles away.
COLLEGE	Make it a fiver, old boy.
MAN	Why?
COLLEGE	I only travel first class.

(With a groan the man complies)

INTERVIEWER	*What a charming young lady . . .*
MANDY	*Thank you.*
INTERVIEWER	*Tell me, do you believe in extra sensory perception.*
MANDY	*Oh, yes, I do. I'm rather psychic myself.*
INTERVIEWER	*Can you give me an example?*
MANDY	*Well, the very first time I met my boyfriend, I knew instinctively that we were completely compatible.*
INTERVIEWER	*You mean, you sensed there was something between you?*
MANDY	*. . . Pardon?*
INTERVIEWER	*You immediately felt his vibrations?*
MANDY	*Ooh, you are awful . . . But I like you!*

MANDY

Mandy

Mandy

Dare I admit that I have no great love for the female characters I portray? At the very least, I am conscious of a sharp edge to my projection of them all. I never present a 'nice' woman, perhaps because deep inside I resent the suggestion that I am a female impersonator. And of all my characters, Mandy is the least real to me. Everything about her seems larger than life. Whereas the others are genuine people, she remains a theatrical figure. However, it is seldom that she does not encroach upon my own life, for all her unreality—she is rather difficult to live with, because wherever I go, someone is always ready with her punchline.

The character was created on an improvised stage in the back of a military lorry during one of our Gang Shows in Normandy in the war. We had to play all the parts between us, male and female. The boys used to like a sing-song, and it fell to my lot to dress up in a blond wig and a full-skirted, giant-polka-dotted dress, and sing 'Under the Old Apple Tree' in a suitably coy way. Those improvised stages seem a far cry from the polished studio floors on which I perform now! At that time, she didn't have a name, but much later I christened her Mandy after a rather notorious young lady who was for a time very much in the news.

When played in the theatre, Mandy becomes almost a pantomime dame figure. Her make-up and clothes have to be so exaggerated, and her voice, instead of coyly fluttering into microphones

113

which pick up the huskiest of whispers, has to make itself heard across the auditorium and above the audience's laughter. You try, if you're male, whispering coy replies so that they're still audible to the back row of a theatre audience! So I generally have to slip in and out of character in order to deliver the punchlines in my own voice to give them emphasis, and Mandy thus comes over as a much harder character.

Her clothes have become quite a feature of each programme, and each dress, though enormously costly, is taken to pieces after the show to prevent its reappearance on another programme. I don't have to be fitted for these creations: so well-oiled is the production machine that I don't even have to try on the dress until we're ready to start filming.

There are grave limits to what can be done with this character. The pattern is too well established to change now, and there is little room for development.

I am always amazed at the extent of Mandy's popularity and renown: she has been featured on the cover of *Punch* magazine and in the *Observer* Supplement, and she was even interviewed by *Nova* on her make-up. Despite my own feelings about the unreality of Mandy, she seems to have achieved an identity of her own. Her success guarantees her a permanent place in the show, of course, but there are times when I wish I could drop her—people are too ready to offer me not just the punchline, but the punch as well! And that reminds me—I once dislocated the poor interviewer's shoulder with a rather too enthusiastic punch! It just goes to show how dangerous it is to tangle with blondes!

INTERVIEWER	*Now here comes a charming young lady.*
MANDY	*Hullo.*
INTERVIEWER	*Tell me, do you have good neighbours?*
MANDY	*Well, I live in a hostel for young ladies. The girls are ever so friendly but we're having trouble with the landlord.*
INTERVIEWER	*Really, what about?*
MANDY	*He objects to us having pin-ups on the wall.*
INTERVIEWER	*So are you girls going to give in and take them down for him?*
MANDY	*Pardon?*
INTERVIEWER	*Or are you going to hang on to yours and stop him tearing them off?*
MANDY	*Ooh, you are awful . . . but I like you!*

INTERVIEWER	*Excuse me.*
MANDY	*Yes?*
INTERVIEWER	*Here's a charming young lady. Tell me, are you impressed by aristocratic titles?*
MANDY	*Oh, no. I speak my mind, no matter who I'm talking to.*
INTERVIEWER	*I see, you mean you wouldn't let anyone take advantage of you?*
MANDY	*Pardon?*
INTERVIEWER	*I mean, you wouldn't take things lying down, even from a duke?*
MANDY	*Ooh, you are awful . . . But I like you!*

THE VICAR

The Vicar

The Vicar

Television vicars—have you noticed them? To me, they are a breed apart, totally divorced from reality. I have watched them intoning the same old pious platitudes in late-night discussion programmes, Sunday religious broadcasts and the nightly epilogues, in voices which must surely be reserved for their TV appearances. I mean, imagine them asking someone to pass the marmalade or scolding the cat, in those precious, measured and holy tones! And what they are actually saying quite passes me by—not because I don't believe in the existence of a Supreme Being, but because I find myself mesmerized into speculation about what they are like when they get home and take off their clerical gear.

The Vicar reflects my impression of the insincerity of the standard TV clergyman. He has the same pious voice and expression, which in his case mask a very disreputable character. He also has a set of protruding front teeth which, admittedly, immediately make him a comic character, but I think, too, that they help him achieve that sanctimonious, butter-wouldn't-melt-in-my-mouth look. For instance, having inadvertently disclosed his true nature while answering the interviewer's questions, he has to compose his features around these teeth in order to resume the usual expression of bland piety which he presents to the world.

We were once encamped on a Sunday in a fashionable West London square for a full day's filming. I was all dressed up as the

Vicar, ready to be filmed against the background of a nearby church, when something went wrong with the sound equipment. While someone was sent back to the TV Centre to fetch a new tape, I was left kicking my heels outside the church in full clerical garb. To my relief, no churchgoers appeared, and I was just beginning to think I'd get by unnoticed when I looked up to see rows and rows of smiling nuns' faces at the window of an adjacent building. Minutes later they were outside and surrounding me. Overcoming our mutual shyness, we began to talk, and several produced cameras and snapped each other standing beside me in my clerical outfit.

To passers-by, we must have looked like a religious convention taking time off to relax — while those nuns who didn't recognize me were completely puzzled as to why their sisters were behaving so strangely about a perfectly ordinary vicar!

I hope I don't give the impression that I am cocking a snook at the Christian religion in my characterization of the Vicar. Far from it. What I try to bring out in the character (in a very exaggerated way, of course) is the patent insincerity which I feel underlies many of its ministers. It seems to me that they are becoming more like show-business performers in their attempts to increase their following, and nowhere is this more apparent than in the religious programmes on television.

Where did I find my Vicar? The truth is, dear viewer, he has been making regular appearances in your home with far longer runs than my series! Study a few of these TV vicars, and see if you can spot the similarities.

One character who has not yet appeared in the shows, but who played a part in my recent film, is Mr Partridge, a solicitor. He is an extension of the Vicar character, and really does belong in the rogues' gallery. Like the Vicar, he has the slick manner of his trade, which masks heaven-knows-what beneath. I find solicitors in general very disconcerting. They hide so much behind their correctly sober suits, impassive expressions and legal jargon, I feel helpless in their hands.

Partridge wears the conventional city suit, old-fashioned wing-collar and bowler hat, and a pair of rimless specs which are in fact my own. He has a habit of screwing up his eyes in a speculative way, and like the Vicar, has protruding teeth which give him a

Mr Partridge ▶

Mr. Partridge

ghastly, sinister leer. Revolting to relate, his finishing touch is a wart on his nose, complete with hair in the centre!

Perhaps we'll be seeing more of this conniving gentleman in future shows.

INTERVIEWER	*Excuse me, Vicar.*
VICAR	*Yes, my son?*
INTERVIEWER	*As a man of the Church, I am sure you have the interests of the community very much at heart.*
VICAR	*Oh, yes indeed. For instance, on behalf of my flock I have been keeping a critical eye on some of the scandalous strip clubs in the neighbourhood.*
INTERVIEWER	*And what are your conclusions?*
VICAR	*Well, for my money you can't whack Miss Lulu and her trained python at the Girlies Galore.*

SCENE: The combined hall and sitting-room of an expensively converted country cottage. Clive Smythe, a distinguished-looking man in his late forties, is opening a bottle of champagne. Other bottles are lined up on the sideboard behind him, together with several silver trays of cocktail snacks.

CLIVE   (calling) Audrey? Come on, old thing.

(A door on the left opens and Audrey enters. She is an attractive woman in a smart day dress)

AUDREY   (roguishly) Clive, what are you up to? (She puts an arm round his waist)

CLIVE   I thought we'd have a little drinkies on our own, darling, before the others arrive. (He hands one of the glasses to Audrey. They raise them to each other with fond smiles) To us, sweetheart. (They clink glasses and drink)

AUDREY   (with a contented sigh) Twenty-five years ago and three grown children. It just doesn't seem possible.

CLIVE   And you're as beautiful now, darling, as you were on our wedding day. I say, let's get rid of our guests as soon as we can, old girl. I thought we might er . . . have a little nap this afternoon, eh?

AUDREY   (in mock reproof) Clive, we've been married twenty-five years, you naughty boy.

(There is a ring at the doorbell)

CLIVE   (putting down his glass and straightening his tie) Ah, that'll be the first of them now. (He goes to the front door and flings it open) Welcome, wel— (He breaks off as he finds himself confronted by Dick, who is wearing his 'Vicar's' teeth, a long, worn raincoat, and a sweat-stained trilby. He looks up at Clive with a creepy smile)

CLIVE   (brusquely) Yes? What do you want?

VICAR   Do I have the honour of addressing Mr Smythe? Mr Clive Smythe, MP?

CLIVE   Yes.

VICAR   Oh, thank heavens.

(He attempts to walk in but Clive throws out an arm and prevents him)

CLIVE   Look here, who are you?

VICAR   (shaking his head sadly) You don't recognise me, do you?

CLIVE   No, I don't.

(The Vicar surveys him sorrowfully, takes off his hat, produces a dirty white handkerchief and puts it round his neck like a clerical collar)

VICAR   (intoning) And now, let us sing number 46, Hymns Ancient and Modern, 'Behold the Bridegroom draweth nigh . . .'

CLIVE   (his jaw dropping) Good grief! It's . . . er . . . (He snaps his fingers, groping for the name) Chislet . . . the Reverend Chislet!

VICAR   One and the same.

CLIVE   This is quite extraordinary. Do come in, please.

126

(The Vicar enters and Clive shuts the door behind him)

CLIVE   Audrey, look who's here. It's the Reverend Chislet.

AUDREY   Oh, I say! How nice. Do have a glass of champagne, Vicar.

CLIVE   You'll hardly believe this, Reverend, but do you know what day this is?

VICAR   Yes. It's the twenty-fifth anniversary of your wedding.

AUDREY   *(handing a glass to the Vicar)* What a fantastic memory!

VICAR   Thank you, dear lady. *(He takes a swift gulp)*

CLIVE   Yes, quite incredible. *(Clive has become aware of the Vicar's somewhat shabby appearance. He eyes him up and down)* Tell me, er . . . are you still at St Luke's, then, Reverend?

VICAR   Alas, no.

AUDREY   Oh.

CLIVE   Was there some . . . er . . . trouble?

VICAR   Well, there was that little incident that took place in the organ loft.

CLIVE   Really?

VICAR   Yes. The Lady Organist swore blind that I'd interfered with her vox humana during Evensong.

CLIVE   Good Lord!

VICAR   But I can assure you I merely trod on her treadle to help her get the wind up her pipes.

AUDREY   How unfortunate.

(She throws a significant glance at Clive and makes a 'get rid of him' gesture behind the Vicar's back. Clive starts to move towards the door. The Vicar stays firmly rooted)

CLIVE   Well, jolly nice of you to pop in, Reverend. You must call again sometime.

AUDREY   Yes, for our Diamond Wedding, perhaps.

VICAR   By the way, may I enquire, has the union been blessed?

CLIVE   Oh, yes, very fruitful. We've three strapping kids.

VICAR   Ah, poor little baskets.

CLIVE   Yes, they certainly . . . what? What did you say?

VICAR   I said . . . poor little baskets.

(Clive moves towards the Vicar with narrowed eyes)

AUDREY   What do you mean? What are you getting at?

VICAR   That, my dear Miss Fairbanks, is the crutch of the matter.

CLIVE   Miss . . . Fairbanks??

VICAR   When you stood before me, twenty-five years ago, to be joined together in Holy Wedlock, it was nothing but a mockery.

CLIVE	What do you mean?
VICAR	Well, for a kick-off—I was never ordained.
AUDREY	You weren't . . . a vicar?
VICAR	No.
CLIVE	So we're not . . . ?
VICAR	I'm afraid not. *(Pause)* Poor little baskets.
AUDREY	*(shouting)* Don't keep saying that!
CLIVE	You swine!
VICAR	Now, now. We must face the world together and purge our souls. Make a clean . . . bosom of it.
CLIVE	*(furious)* Don't you drag us into it.
VICAR	But you are already in it, Mr Smythe. Up to there. After all, for the past twenty-five years you have been living together . . . in sin.

(Clive and Audrey stare at each other in horror. Audrey lets out a sudden shriek and clouts Clive across the cheek)

AUDREY	You beast!
CLIVE	Why me?
AUDREY	I've just remembered last night. You seducer, you!
CLIVE	My God, I've just remembered something, too. The Party Chairman's coming today to talk about that new appointment of mine.
VICAR	One to which you will bring your undoubted talents, I trust?
CLIVE	*(savagely)* Oh, yes. It's Chairman of the Council for Unmarried Mothers.
VICAR	Ah, in that case, may I submit for your consideration the case of Miss Fairbanks here, and her three little toddlers?
AUDREY	*(sobbing)* How could you do this to me?
VICAR	Pray don't upset yourself, dear lady. Confession is good for the soul. Once the . . . somewhat unpleasant newspaper publicity has died down—and your dear husband is released from prison . . .
CLIVE	Prison? What do you mean, prison?
VICAR	The Inland Revenue don't take kindly to persons who claim for a wife and three children when they're not even married.
CLIVE	I promise you one thing, if I go to prison, I'll make sure you do too.
VICAR	I have already done my porridge—it's the Big Beak in the sky I'm worried about. By the way, if you get a choice, do plump for Parkhurst, the sea air is so bracing.

(Clive starts to laugh semi-hysterically)

AUDREY	I don't know what you can find to laugh at.

CLIVE I'm thinking of the fuss your sanctimonious mother kicked up when young Charlie was born seven months after the wedding. Little does she know the other two are a pair of bast . . .! *(He hastily claps his hand over his mouth)*

AUDREY You callous beast!

CLIVE *(sobering rapidly)* You're right.

(There is a ring at the doorbell. Clive and Audrey freeze in terror. The Vicar looks from one to the other)

VICAR *(benignly)* Shall I go?

CLIVE No, no! You're here to read the meter, understand?

(He opens the door to reveal a ferrety little man with a note-pad in his hand. He raises his hat)

MAN Good morning. Mr Clive Smythe?

CLIVE No. That is to say—yes.

MAN I'm from the *Morning Argus*. I understand it's your Silver Wedding and I wonder if I could . . .

(The Vicar rushes towards the door)

VICAR Don't say a word! *(He glares at the reporter)* Wrong house. *(He slams the door)*

CLIVE Well, at least that was decent of you. We want to keep this out of the papers.

VICAR We most certainly do. Except the *News of the World*, of course.

CLIVE What??

VICAR Well, I've offered them an exclusive 'True Confessions of a Bogus Priest'—by Ignatius Chislet.

AUDREY I feel faint. Stop him, Clive, stop him!

CLIVE *(grimly)* All right, you putrid parson. How much are they paying you?

VICAR The sum of one thousand pounds was mentioned. Which, I hasten to add, I intend to use for relieving fallen women in Brixton.

CLIVE *(whipping out a cheque book and writing)* I'll give you fifteen hundred. Go to the Bahamas and relieve them.

(The Vicar takes the cheque and blows on it to dry the ink)

CLIVE Right. Now, get out.

VICAR Very well. *(He turns to Audrey)* So nice to have met you again . . . *(he winks conspiratorially)* Mrs Smythe.

(Clive opens the door. The Vicar crosses and pauses in the doorway)

VICAR *(to Clive)* By the way, why don't you ask that dolly little secretary of yours to move in? After all, you're a bachelor.

(As the Vicar exits, a slow smile begins to spread over Clive's face. It rapidly disappears when a plate of smoked salmon sandwiches splatters against the wall by his head.

Outside the front door, the Vicar is joined by the ferret-faced 'reporter')

MAN How did it go, Rev?

VICAR *(showing him the cheque)* Not bad at all, old son. Now, our next call is on Mr and Mrs Seamus O'Reilly of Killarney Cottage.

MAN You never married them, did you?

VICAR No, but when I was Father McGinty I heard some very interesting confessions that should be worth a bob or two.

INTERVIEWER	*Excuse me, Vicar.*
VICAR	*Yes?*
INTERVIEWER	*What do you feel about class distinction?*
VICAR	*I think it is totally wrong. In the eyes of Our Lord all men are created equal, and our behaviour should mirror that thought.*
INTERVIEWER	*In other words, do as you would be done by?*
VICAR	*Oh,* exactly. *And I'd like to do the rotten swine who puts a washer in the plate every Sunday!*

INTERVIEWER	*Excuse me, Vicar . . .*
VICAR	*Good morning, my son.*
INTERVIEWER	*Have you ever had an opportunity and made a decision which turned out for the best?*
VICAR	*Indeed I have. One such springs to mind immediately. I was once in a position to save a young lady of my acquaintance from being amorously assaulted and smothered in violent and passionate kisses.*
INTERVIEWER	*And how did you do that?*
VICAR	*I managed to talk myself out of it.*

THE NEIGHBOUR

The Neighbour

Although there is really no such character as the Neighbour, the name has become a term of easy reference to identify the bitchy, always-comes-off-best lady who often appears in the show in situation comedy sketches with Pat Coombs. Whether they are the front and back ends of a pantomime horse, vying to take over the star role, or duchesses, each with a very much less than respectable past, or rival door-to-door saleswomen pushing the same brand of cosmetics, the basic situation is always the same. Pat plays the stooge, the 'nice', gullible, put-upon lady forever desperately trying to hold her own against me—her ruthless, domineering, scheming, sneering companion—and forever losing out.

Because she isn't a consistent character in that she doesn't appear always in one role, there seemed little point in pinning the Neighbour down to one particular aspect of her various guises in a photograph. So, we have chosen instead a script which illustrates exactly the kind of woman she is, in all her nastiness, embodying all the petty vices of spite, envy, malice and jealousy which belong to a truly bad neighbour.

FRIENDS AND NEIGHBOURS

SCENE: *Two back gardens divided by a fence. The garden on the right is neatly kept, with a goldfish pond surrounded by stone gnomes, flowers along the fence and a small rabbit hutch. The garden on the left is a shambles. It is littered with a broken pram, a rusty bicycle frame and a couple of overflowing dustbins. Both gardens have small revolving clothes dryers.*

Dick appears as Ethel the Neighbour in the left-hand garden from the back door of the house. He wears a headscarf over a ginger wig in curlers, a wrap-over floral pinafore, bedroom slippers and wrinkled tights. A cigarette dangles from the corner of 'her' mouth. Under one arm 'she' carries a carrier bag full to the brim with empty beer cans and spirit bottles. With the other hand 'she' propels a rickety pushchair piled with washing. 'She' pauses and shouts through the back door.

ETHEL   Marlon, will you leave Granny alone? And take that apple off her head. She doesn't want to play William Tell. Flaming kid, he'll be the death of me—or Gran.

(She parks the pushchair and moves to the dustbins. Realising that there is no room for the empties, she goes to the fence, glances round to make sure she is unobserved and dumps them into the next door garden. She moves down the fence to where a large marrow is growing. She produces a pair of scissors from the pocket of her pinny, leans over the fence, snips the marrow stem and picks it up. Win appears from the back door of the other house, singing 'I Love Paris in the Springtime'. Ethel hastily shoves the marrow under her pinafore)

ETHEL   Win! Hullo, love. You're back a day early. Well, I never.

WIN   Hullo, Ethel. *Comment ça va?*

ETHEL   Eh?

WIN   Oh. Keep forgetting I'm back in England.

ETHEL   Yes, it must be difficult after a long weekend. Anyway, did you have a nice time?

WIN   Oh, I can't tell you. The South of France—*formidable!*

ETHEL   Whereabouts exactly did you stay?

WIN   Er . . . Venice.

ETHEL   Oh, lovely. I must say, you're looking ever so well. You really have caught the sun.

WIN   Well, they don't call it the Costa del Sol for nothing, you know. You're not looking so . . . *(Her eyes travel down to the protruberance under Ethel's pinny)* Ooh! I say—Ethel, you haven't!

ETHEL   Haven't what, love?

WIN   After all this time—you haven't fallen?

ETHEL   *(looking down uncomfortably)* Oh, no. I ate some home-made bread for breakfast and I think it's still rising.

WIN   Oh well, mustn't stand here gossiping. I've got to get my bits and pieces out.

ETHEL   *(watches her disappear into her back door)* You're a worker. I've always said that. You're a worker.

(She quickly hides the marrow under her washing, then leans through the fence and cuts off a dozen tulips with her scissors. She snatches a piece of newspaper from the dustbin and hastily wraps the flowers as Win reappears carrying a plastic washing basket)

ETHEL   Here you are, dear, I bought you a few flowers as a welcome home present.

136

WIN   *(taking them)* Oh, you are a pet. You're so thoughtful. *(She sniffs them)* Aren't they gorgeous? Just like the ones . . . *(she looks at the empty flower bed)* we used to have down there.

ETHEL   *(starting to hang grubby-looking laundry on her dryer)* Well, I always think of you as almost part of my own family.

WIN   *(also hanging washing)* So do I. Aren't we lucky? Never a cross word.

ETHEL   You know my motto. 'Do unto others . . .' I always say.

WIN   I know, I know.

(Win turns the dryer to bring a sparkling new slip opposite Ethel, who eyes it calculatingly)

ETHEL   You don't have to go to church to be a Christian . . . *(as Win turns away for another piece of laundry, Ethel swipes the slip and replaces it with a tatty one of her own)* all is pure to the pure in heart. *(She flips Win's dryer round so that the tatty slip is out of sight)*

WIN   *(casually)* By the way, did you remember to feed my rabbits?

ETHEL   Er . . . well . . . not exactly.

(Win moves to the hutch and looks inside)

WIN   *(horrified)* My gawd! They've gone! What happened? What?

ETHEL   You're never going to believe this . . .

WIN   Oooh! Oooh, you never! You never ate Eric and Ernie! Oh, I don't know what my Wally'll say. He was so fond of those rabbits he was going to have them stuffed.

ETHEL   They were, dear. With sage and onion.

WIN   By the way, what, may I ask, has happened to my Cox's Orange Pippin?

ETHEL   How do you mean?

WIN   My apple tree. There's not a bit of fruit left on it.

ETHEL   Well, you did say I could have all the windfalls.

WIN   Yes, but I heard nothing on the news about a flaming hurricane.

ETHEL   You wouldn't, dear, would you—in Venice?

WIN   . . . No. I suppose not. Strikes me there's a lot of funny things been going on since I went away.

(Win picks up another piece of washing and swings the dryer to find a vacant space for it. This brings a bra opposite Ethel, who promptly swipes it)

ETHEL   Oh? And what does that remark mean?

WIN   I'm not blind, you know. Those empty bottles weren't there last week. How do you account for those?

137

ETHEL My lips are sealed. If you can't say anything good about a person, keep your mouth shut. It was your lodger.

WIN Mr Owen? I can't believe it. Why, he's a Major in the Salvation Army.

ETHEL Yes, but it isn't half thirsty work banging that big drum.

BOY *(offstage)* Mum?

ETHEL Yes, Marlon?

BOY *(offstage)* The landlord's here for the rent.

ETHEL Send him through, dear. *(To Win)* Here, are you in for a shock!

WIN Why? What do you mean?

ETHEL While you were away, the landlord's gone berserk. He's doubled the rents.

WIN What??? After Wal and me had the whole house redecorated out of our own pockets!

ETHEL I know, and 'No pets' he says. 'No lodgers.' 'No hanging washing outside.'

WIN Who does he think he is? I'll give him a piece of my mind when I see him.

ETHEL Oh, so shall I, love. As long as we stick together he'll have to climb down.

WIN I don't know what I'd do without you, Ethel.

(The landlord appears from Ethel's back door)

LANDLORD *(jocularly)* 'Morning, ladies. Got everything hanging out, I see.

WIN Don't you come here with your filthy remarks, you little bloodsucker! I'd like to hang you out! I'll go to the Tribunal, that'll wipe the smirk off your nasty little face. What have you done about my drains, I ask you? And I'm not having my cat put to sleep for nobody. I'll keep pigs if I want to! Pigs!

(She storms off into the house. The landlord stares after her, open-mouthed. Ethel has been watching the scene with interest. The landlord turns to her)

LANDLORD And all I said was ''Morning, ladies'!

ETHEL What can you expect? *(She nods significantly at the pile of empty bottles in Win's garden)* She don't know what she's saying half the time.

LANDLORD *(gazing at the bottles)* My gawd, I never knew.

ETHEL Well, I'm not one to complain, but it's purgatory living next door to her when she's in her cups.

LANDLORD I've a good mind to give her a week's notice.

ETHEL I wouldn't blame you. I wouldn't blame you. If her house does fall vacant I suppose there's no chance of me moving in?

LANDLORD Well, there's no harm in talking about it.

ETHEL Over a nice cup of tea and a little snack. You go in and tell Gran to put the kettle on. I won't be a minute.

(The landlord disappears into the house. Ethel picks up a large shrimping net on a long pole, leans over the fence and scoops out Win's goldfish pond. She holds up the net and looks at the fish in it)

ETHEL   Yes, sardines on toast, I think. *(She exits into the house)*

Postscript

So, now you have seen how a few of my characters have originated and developed. They have become my closest friends, so to speak, and are people whose reactions I can trust.

I can wait in the wings feeling pretty low-spirited, and even unwell, but the moment dear old Lampwick *et al* shuffle, mince, teeter, strut or swagger out from behind the set, the warmth of the audience lifts me, and I am taken out of myself completely and into character. There have been many ups and downs over the years, and my characters have been with me and seen me through them all. I consider myself truly fortunate in that they at least are one set of companions who will stay with me for ever.